GREAT
for GOD

DAVID SHIBLEY

First printing: April 2012

New Leaf Press, P.O. Box 726, Green Forest, AR 72638

New Leaf Press is a division of the New Leaf Publishing Group, Inc.

ISBN: 978-0-89221-709-0
Library of Congress Catalog Number: 2012935000

Cover image: Peeter Viisimaa, Getty Images
Interior images: Global Advance: 9, 15, 27, 31, 61, 83, 95, 125
Shutterstock.com: 15, 19, 27, 31, 35, 41, 45, 49, 53, 57, 61, 65, 69, 73, 79, 83, 89, 95, 99, 105, 111, 117, 121

Please consider requesting that a copy of this volume be purchased by your local library system.

Printed in the United States of America

Please visit our website for other great titles:
www.newleafpress.net

For information regarding author interviews, please contact the publicity department at (870) 438-5288.

New Leaf Press
A Division of New Leaf Publishing Group

To be called to a life of extraordinary quality, to live up to it, and yet to be unconscious of it is indeed a narrow way.

Dietrich Bonhoeffer
The Cost of Discipleship

Most people plot and plan themselves into mediocrity, while now and again somebody forgets himself into greatness.

E. Stanley Jones
Abundant Living

Forbid that we should ever consider the holding of a commission from the King of kings a sacrifice, so long as other men esteem the service of an earthly government as an honor. I am a missionary, heart and soul. God Himself had an only Son, and He was a missionary and physician. A poor, poor imitation I am, or wish to be, but in this service I hope to live. In it I wish to die. I still prefer poverty and missions service to riches and ease. This is my choice.

David Livingstone

Acknowledgments

First and foremost, I'm grateful to my wife, Naomi. She is my beautiful partner in life and ministry. Throughout much of the holidays I was tucked away in my study or researching in seminary libraries. Naomi didn't complain. She believes in the mission and ministry of this book. It never would have been completed without her support and encouragement. To see our sons embrace the call of the Great Commission (Jonathan as president of Global Advance and Joel as a Christ-honoring businessman) is a great joy to us both.

I'm grateful to Tim Dudley, president of New Leaf Publishing Group, who believed in me as an author and helped resurrect this avenue of ministry for me. Laura Welch, my editor, and the entire team at New Leaf have done an excellent job.

Much of the biographical information has come from Ruth Tucker's voluminous research. She has chronicled the advance of the gospel through human instruments in her epic book, *From Jerusalem to Irian Jaya*.

When I was a young preacher, four professors helped ground me in a solid theology that is both evangelical and evangelistic: Andrew Bowling and Jim Walters at John Brown University and James Eaves and Roy Fish at Southwestern Baptist Theological Seminary.

I gratefully acknowledge three men who were profoundly involved in shaping my missiology. My dad, the late Warren Shibley, modeled sacrificial giving and a heart for the world. T. L. Osborn conducted nation-shaking evangelistic meetings that introduced vast multitudes to the living Christ. I share the opinion of the president of Southwestern Seminary that the late Cal Guy, my missions professor and a member of the International Mission Board for Southern Baptists, was "the greatest missions professor in the world." Dr. Guy championed the cause of the indigenous church and the raising up of national leaders to reach their own people and surrounding peoples with the gospel.

This emphasis on equipping those we call *frontline shepherds* led to the founding of Global Advance. I am humbled and honored to serve with Global Advance's staff, international representatives, volunteers, and partners in bringing Jesus global glory and helping to fulfill His Great Commission.

Last but by no means least, our personal prayer team, led by Roger and Charlotte Merschbrock, literally prayed me across the finish line in writing this project. Here is your faith made sight.

CONTENTS

NEEDED: LEADERS WHO ARE GREAT FOR GOD

You can be great for God.

You should be great for God.

Our times beg you to be great for God.

You and this book have met at just the right moment.

A call to greatness in no way contradicts the strong teachings of Scripture regarding humility and servanthood. It does require that our definitions of *greatness* and *success* be biblical. Jesus' view of greatness stands in polar antithesis to the world's view. "You know that those who are considered rulers over the Gentiles lord it over them," He said, "and their great ones exercise authority over them. Yet it shall not be so among you; but whoever desires to become great among you shall be your servant" (Mark 10:42–43). Only servants can lead in His kingdom.

Christ's servants today stand on the shoulders of His servants of earlier eras whose lives were often packed with more adventure than the most riveting novel. The profiles in this book will introduce you to the extraordinary lives of servants who shook the world. Their greatness had little to do with status, wealth, or acclaim (all of which they often lacked). Yet their lives soared above mediocrity, lifted millions, and brought great glory to God.

You will read how a campus Christian meeting changed everything for a young dreamer named John R. Mott. That pivotal night at Cornell, Mott heard a renowned missionary issue this challenge: "Young man, seekest thou great things for thyself? Seek them not! "Seek first the kingdom of God" (see Jer. 45:5 and Matt. 6:33).[1] Suddenly everything inside this college student snapped to attention. From that night, his focus was clear. He would be great because he would tether his life to a great Lord and His great cause.

Such defining points mark us and shape our future. The subjects of this book were visionary, motivated, and imperfect. They sought great things — *but not for themselves.* They were great *for God.* They lived out William Carey's daring challenge, "Expect great things from God; attempt great things for God."[2]

Christ's servants never pursue greatness for its own sake. Those who are great for God are passionate about God and His purposes. The end game is God's glory and advancing His kingdom. Their lives point past themselves to a great Redeemer. They echo the prophet's desire for the fame of His name: "Your name and renown are the desire of our hearts" (Isa. 26:8; New International Version).

In today's warped world we have traded greatness for mere celebrity. But laurels and limelight are never at the forefront of those who are great for God. You will see in the lives of these great servants a refreshing disregard and distrust of accolades. One can only imagine what their reaction would be to today's fixation with celebrities. No doubt they would have labeled it real, repugnant idolatry. We all appreciate affirmation, but the applause these great ones sought most was the applause of heaven.

You will witness true humility on every page of their stories. Most of these men and women were from common stock. They knew their disproportionate impact came not by might or human ingenuity but by God's Spirit (see Zech 4:6). At some point they shifted beyond their best efforts to the overdrive of supernatural power. Confidence in their calling and in who they were in Christ saved them from the dual ditches of pride and low self-esteem.

Their allegiance was to Jesus with hearts bowed in worship and wills poised to obey. Like John, they pointed people to God's Lamb (John 1:29, 36). And with John they confessed, "He must increase, but I must decrease" (John 3:30).

I am not given to hyperbole. I am sure that your interaction with the great lives chronicled in this book will change your life. Your life will be enriched. The book in your hands holds big benefits for you.

Reading the stories of these great lives will encourage you. The Bible says, "One generation shall praise Your works to another, and shall declare Your mighty acts" (Ps. 145:4). The record of the global advance of the Christian faith is one of the most thrilling sagas in all history. Often it has been written in blood. I felt a debt to the next generation to pass on these stories of courageous, even audacious, faith. Everyone deserves to hear the awesome accounts you are about to read. These stories are just too wonderful to die, and these people are too great to be forgotten. In a time when hope is in short supply, you will gain fresh incentive in your own fight of faith as you relate to the trials and triumphs of those who have gone before you.

Reading the stories of these great lives will enlighten you. "Histories make men wise," wrote Francis Bacon.[3] To comprehend our times we must know how we arrived in them. Now, in my sixties, it grieves me to see the same avoidable errors committed trans-generationally. The old adage that those who do not learn from history are doomed to repeat it is painfully true. Our world may seem light years removed from the world of many of these heroes of faith but their challenges are ours, as well. Human frailty, personality conflicts, spiritual battles, heroism, defeats, and victories — these themes transcend the boundaries of generations. Further, we are strengthened by knowing God's unfailing faithfulness that sustained them will sustain us (see 1 Cor. 10:13).

Reading the stories of these great lives will enlarge you. These stories will make your heart bigger. And once expanded, your heart will never be content to retreat to its former size. Your bigger perspective will call you to bigger choices. The nobility of these lives force upon us weighty questions like those posed by pastor-theologian

James Emery White: "Do we mark our years by dedication to God and his eternal purposes, or do we strip our lives of any sense of calling and answer only to the voice of an autonomous individualism? Do we live in light of the great redemptive drama, selflessly giving ourselves to the advance of the kingdom and the building of the Church, or do we find ourselves drifting into a narcissistic hedonism that makes all spiritual alignments a consumer affair?"[4]

Frankly, this book should come with a red-letter warning. If you interface with these great lives you will inevitably reach a crossroads. At that juncture you will make a pivotal choice: Will you consign yourself to a little life or will you be great for God? Your decision carries huge consequences — for you and for your generation. If you take "the road less traveled," that will make all the difference.[5]

Reading the stories of these great lives will provide examples for you. Without a hint of arrogance Paul could confidently say, "Follow my example, as I follow the example of Christ" (1 Cor 11:1; NIV). While we do not seek to imitate these pioneers, we do seek to mirror their example as devoted Christ-followers. They carried the spirit of the ancient sons of Issachar. They understood their times, but they were not just social analysts. Their discernment prompted action — they knew what God's people should do in light of their times (1 Chron. 12:32). How desperately we need such perceptive, purposeful leaders today.

This book will impact both individuals and groups. I hope you will read it alone, just God and you. Also, I hope it will be used in Bible studies, classrooms, and in family devotions. These stories are ideal to be read aloud at family times around the table or to be read pensively by a warm fire.

One of the toughest issues in crafting this book was deciding who to leave out. Those options were made a little easier by writing only about people who are already with the Lord in heaven. That way I didn't have to choose among the wonderful people faithfully serving Christ today. But there are thousands of unsung heroes, people just as great or greater than the ones you will read about. Heaven has recorded each of their stories. One day we will hear them all.

These great lives tug at something deep inside us. "Deep calls unto deep" (Ps. 42:7). The lives of these flawed yet great servant-leaders impel us to be "our utmost for His highest."[6] You probably picked up this book because you want your life to count. It is for you this book was written. You have stepped onto the stage of God's unfolding global drama "for such a time as this" (Esther 4:14). You were born on purpose. You were born again on purpose. You were born at this time on purpose.

In this epochal era of world and church history, may you be great for God. May you advance His purposes in your times. A life that is great for God is a life that merits Jesus' approval. I pray this book moves you to live this day in light of That Day, just as these great ones lived.[7] And on That Day may you hear the words to be prized above life itself: "Well done, good and faithful servant" (Matt. 25:21, 23).

CHAPTER 1

PRESS ON

Missionary	Rowland Victor Bingham
Birth	1872 in Sussex, England
Death	1942 in Toronto, Canada
Legacy	Over 10,000 came to faith in Christ and 1,000 churches were planted as a result of Roland Bingham's pioneering ministry in Africa. He founded the Sudan Interior Mission (now known SIM International). SIM is active in 50 nations among people groups in Africa, Asia, and South America.
Quote	It is fashionable in the Western world to relegate belief in demons and devils to the realm of mythology, and when mentioned at all it is in jest. But it is no jest in West Africa or any other mission field for that matter.

And so I have made it my aim to preach the gospel, not where Christ was named, lest I should build on another man's foundation, but as it is written: "To whom He was not announced, they shall see; and those who have not heard shall understand" (Rom. 15:20–21).

Rowland Bingham was heard to say, "I will open Africa to the gospel or die trying." He nearly died trying. But amidst the pain of friends' deaths and against seemingly insurmountable odds, Rowland succeeded in establishing the Sudan Interior Mission and bringing the good news to the people of the Sudan.

Rowland Bingham had a happy childhood in Sussex, England. When he was 13 years old, however, life changed dramatically. Bingham's father died, and Rowland had to work full-time. He received Christ as his Savior through the Salvation Army and began his lifelong walk with the Lord. While still a teenager, Rowland was drawn to opportunities offered in the New World. Not long after his move to Canada, God called him to preach. Soon he was an officer in the Salvation Army. But through contact with an elderly, praying woman named Mrs. Gowans, Bingham's life would be pointed toward Africa. Mrs. Gowan's son Walter had studied special needs in the world. From this he decided the people of the Sudan in central Africa were some of the world's neediest. Sixty million people there had no Christian witness. Through talks and prayer with Walter's mother, Bingham became convinced that he should join Walter in attempting to reach the Sudan with the gospel.

In 1893, while in his early twenties, Bingham sailed with a college friend, Thomas Kent, to join Walter on his journey. Filled with excitement, they were stopped short when they arrived in Nigeria. "Young men, you will never see the Sudan," the head of a missions agency told them. "Your children will never see the Sudan; your grandchildren may." This disheartening warning seemed true, for Bingham soon became ill and had to remain in West Africa while the other two left on their 800-mile journey to the Sudan. Within a year, both were dead. Walter Gowans was captured by a tribal chieftain and though he was later released, he died from a weakened physical condition. Thomas Kent died of the effects of malaria.

After hearing of the deaths of his friends, Bingham returned to England heartbroken. He began to search his heart to be sure of his call. "My faith was being shaken to the very foundation," he later declared. "For months the struggle over this great issue went on before I was finally brought back to the solid rock."[1]

Realizing his need for more training for missions work, he took a basic medical course and then enrolled in a Bible school in New York City headed by A.B. Simpson. While a student there, he pastored a small church, but his heart continued to burn for the Sudan. It was too dear a price to pay not to win someday.

In 1898, Bingham married Helen Blair. He also started the Sudan Interior Mission to raise funds for another try at opening that region to the Christian message. In 1900 Bingham launched his second attempt to reach the Sudan. Again he found the missionaries in West Africa had no sympathy with his hopes. Again Bingham was struck down with malaria and

“There is the constant spiritual warfare that has to be waged against the powers of darkness.”

~ ROWLAND BINGHAM ~

had to return home. His companions on this trip, though promising to continue, lost heart. They, too, returned home. After this second failure, Bingham recalled, "I went through the darkest period of my life." Still, Bingham refused to give up. Gathering four more recruits in Canada, he made a third attempt the next year. This time he succeeded. He started the first Sudan Interior Mission (SIM) station at Patigi, 500 miles up the Niger River from the coast. At first, Rowland encountered the same problems he had before. He saw only a few converted to Christ. And within four years, only one of his four helpers remained: one had died and two were sent home, too ill ever to return.

He did finally begin to see the fruit of his perseverance when he started new missionary stations that gave SIM a foothold in the region. A cure for malaria was found, which helped mission recruits live longer in the region. But more than anything else, Bingham and his assistants learned to pray with power. "There is the constant invisible warfare," Bingham wrote, "that has to be waged against the powers of darkness." Over the years, the Sudan Interior Mission would start hundreds of churches. Missionaries established Bible schools for the training of Sudanese pastors. And the SIM built medical centers and became a primary force in the fight to rid Africa of the dreaded disease of leprosy.

When he was 69 years old, Bingham was amazed at the expansion of the gospel throughout the Sudan. Although the Christians were often tortured and even killed for their faith, the church continued to grow. Bingham had just completed a book about 50 years of life with the SIM in Africa when he died, apparently of a heart attack.

Nevertheless, Bingham had lived to see 10,000 people converted to Christ and nearly 1,000 churches planted through SIM. Often the difference between success or failure lies in the ability to keep on trying. Rowland did what righteous people do, according to Scripture: "Though a righteous man falls seven times, he rises again" (Prov. 24:16; NIV). It was one of the greatest success stories of Christian missions in African history, all because one man would not give up.

CHAPTER 2

CHRIST'S SLAVE

Mission Leader	William R. (Bill) Bright
Birth	1921 in Coweta, Oklahoma
Death	2003 in Orlando, Florida
Legacy	Bill Bright founded Campus Crusade for Christ, one of the largest Christian ministries in the world with multi-faceted outreaches in 191 nations. He wrote some 100 books and numerous pamphlets and articles. His printed presentation of the gospel, *Do You Know the Four Spiritual Laws?* has been disseminated to over 2.5 billion people. He was the visionary and primary fund raiser for the *JESUS* film, the most successful evangelistic tool in church history. In 1996 Bright received the Templeton Prize for Progress in Religion for his research that helped ignite a prayer and fasting awakening among Christians worldwide.
Quote	I have known for many years now that I have salvation in Jesus, and that I am filled with and controlled by the Holy Spirit, living in the center of God's will, fully surrendered to the Lordship of Christ. This confidence is necessary for godly leadership.

Those who are wise shall shine like the brightness of the firmament, and those who turn many to righteousness like the stars forever and ever (Daniel 12:3).

The founder of the world's largest ministry stood before hundreds of younger church leaders. Bill Bright looked at us and said, "For the last 50 years, I have made every decision in light of this question — *how will this decision affect the fulfilling of the Great Commission?*"

It was 1988 and my wife, Naomi, and I were delegates to Leadership '88, a historic conference for younger church leaders. We were humbled to be seated at a dinner table with Bill Bright and his wife, Vonette. At the time I was 38 and thrilled to be with these giants of the faith. When I heard his statement I immediately thought, *what a testimony*. Had almost anyone else made that statement, it would have seemed pretentious. From Bill Bright it was a factual, powerful statement of a life commitment. He was a missionary statesman of the first order.

William R. Bright was born in the small east Oklahoma town of Coweta on October 19, 1921, the sixth of seven children. His mother had lost a previous son at childbirth. While pregnant with Bill she was told her own life was at risk. The doctor expressed little hope that both she and the baby could make it. It was then that Mary Lee Bright prayed and made a promise to God to dedicate her child to His service. Only decades later, after he came to faith in Christ, did his mother reveal her promise to Bill.

Throughout his youth Bill was, in his words, a "happy pagan." A local minister had an adulterous affair that turned him in disgust from his Christian upbringing. "I set my goals as a humanist, materialist, self-sufficient person — no God, no Savior, and no Bible."[1]

Bill was a junior in college when the Japanese launched the deadly attack on Pearl Harbor in 1941, forcing a reluctant United States into World War II. The day after the attack Bill practically begged recruiters to be enlisted with the armed forces in the war effort, but he was rejected because of a perforated eardrum. He graduated from Northeastern State University in Tahlequah, Oklahoma, in 1943 with an economics degree. After a brief stint teaching, Bill determined he could serve his country best as a successful businessman.

Soon after graduation he headed to California for something — anything — bigger than what he considered the stifling confines of small-town Oklahoma. Bill's first night in California proved to be a night of miracles, and the start of the answer to his mother's prayers for Bill's conversion. A casual talk with a young man on a Los Angeles street corner led to Bill going to a Bible study at the home of Dawson Trotman, hoping he could spend the night there. Just a few years later these two young men would be heading two fruitful, robust ministries and reshaping the image of evangelical Christianity.[2]

And so it was that on his first night in Los Angeles young Bill Bright received Dawson Trotman's hospitality. At a birthday party after the Bible study Bill met Dan Fuller, son of the radio evangelist Charles E. Fuller. God had already begun to orchestrate the steps of Bill Bright.

A decade after that God-ordained night, Trotman's Navigators were in a race against time to purchase Glen Eyrie, their proposed Colorado headquarters. Bill Bright, by then founder of the fledgling Campus Crusade for Christ, personally gave sacrificially and wrote 5,000 friends of his new organization, asking them to help, saying he wanted to return the kindness Dawson had shown him. With Bill's help, the Navigators were able to purchase the property.[3]

Bill founded Bright's California Confectionaries and quickly became successful selling candied fruits and nuts. To enhance his social circle he began attending the First Presbyterian Church in Hollywood. There he met the legendary Christian educator Dr. Henrietta Mears. Through her influence Bill committed his life to Christ in 1945. Bill soon became part of a small Bible study in her home. He furthered his training by studying at Princeton Seminary, then later enrolling in the first class of the new Fuller Theological Seminary.

Largely through Dr. Mears's influence, his friend since childhood, Vonette Zachary, also gave her life to Christ. The long friendship of Bill and Vonette had blossomed into love. They grew in their new faith as part of Dr. Mears's weekly meeting, the Fellowship of the Burning Heart. Bill and Vonette were married on December 30, 1948. Together they became one of the most influential couples in Christian leadership. They had two sons. Today, both sons are serving Christ; Zachary is a pastor and Brad serves on the staff of Campus Crusade.

On a Sunday afternoon in the spring of 1951, Bill and Vonette wrote formal contracts, renouncing control of anything and giving themselves voluntarily to be slaves of Jesus Christ. Within a week of this total commitment as a slave of Christ, Bill had a dramatic encounter with God. Studying for final exams at seminary about midnight he envisioned a panoramic view of fulfilling Christ's Great Commission. The focal point of this global mission would be reaching college students with the gospel. "God met with me," Bill said. "He gave me my marching orders. He told me what I was to do in broad strokes as on an artist's canvas. That night He gave me the broad picture of the world."[4] Bill shared this vision with one of his seminary professors, the renowned Bible teacher Wilbur M. Smith. The next day in class, Dr. Smith handed Bill a note with what he believed should be the name of the new ministry: Campus Crusade for Christ.

In obedience to this clear call to minister to students, that same year Bill and Vonette launched the first chapter of Campus Crusade for Christ at UCLA, focusing on reaching campus leaders and athletes. This outreach began with the belief, "Win the campus to Christ today, win the world to Christ tomorrow." The vision was to "win, build, and send" millions of students to share God's love in Christ first to their campuses and then throughout the world.

By 1960, Campus Crusade for Christ had chapters on 40 campuses across America and had spread to Mexico, Pakistan, and South Korea. Then the growth of the ministry exploded over the next several decades. Campus Crusade rode the crest of the wave of the Jesus Movement of the late 1960s and early 1970s. Many contemporary church historians believe the zenith of the Jesus Movement was Explo '72, spearheaded by Bill Bright and Campus Crusade. Some 80,000 high school and college students overflowed the Cotton Bowl in Dallas to be trained and challenged to reach their campuses with the gospel. Two years later, Explo '74 drew 300,000 attendees in Seoul, South Korea, making it the largest Christian event in history up to that time.

> "We shall see a resurgence in evangelism and a zeal unparalleled in church history as we endeavor — in the power of the Holy Spirit — to help fulfill the Great Commission."
>
> ~ BILL BRIGHT ~

For half a century, Bill Bright built and led Campus Crusade for Christ. By the time he handed over the reins of leadership it was the largest Christian ministry in the world. Today this ministry serves in 191 nations with 26,000 full time employees and more than 225,000 trained volunteers.[5] Many auxiliary ministries have been spawned under the aegis of Campus Crusade, including outreaches to athletes and the military and the ministry of Josh McDowell.

Not only was Bill the visionary leader of a global ministry with a big umbrella, he was one of the most successful fund-raisers ever for Christian causes. Because people knew Bill and Vonette did not live extravagantly (they divested most of their personal assets as part of their contract to be Christ's slaves), there was a high level of trust in giving to the ministry of Campus Crusade for Christ. Grandmothers with small, fixed pensions wanted to help. And Bill convinced a good number of wealthy Christians to be part of "history's handful" who would invest one million dollars for the spread of the gospel.

Bill Bright thought, dreamed, and prayed in world terms. "Small plans cannot enflame the minds of men," he said.[6] All of Bill Bright's evangelistic initiatives were, in a word, *huge*. In 1956 he wrote the gospel tract *The Four Spiritual Laws* which he called "a positive, 20-minute presentation of the claims of Christ: who He is, why He came, and how one can know Him personally."[7] This booklet has been printed in some 200 languages and distributed to over 2.5 billion people, making it the most widely disseminated religious booklet in history.

In 1976 Bill spearheaded the "Here's Life, America" campaign with the goal "to saturate the United States with the gospel." Its slogan, "I found it!" seemed to be everywhere, on billboards, bumper stickers, radio and TV ads, and millions of printed pieces. The high profile given to the gospel resulted in multitudes of new Christian believers.

In 1979 he commissioned the *JESUS* film and became the primary fund-raiser for what would become the single greatest evangelistic tool of the 20th century. At the time of this writing, the *JESUS* film has been translated into 1,121 languages spoken by 91 percent of the world's population, with an estimated 200 million viewers responding to the film by praying to receive Christ as their Savior.[8]

New Life 2000 divided the world into 5,000 regions with populations of one million each, seeking to saturate each region with the *JESUS* film. This was augmented by a massive initiative to get a video copy of the *JESUS* film into every home in the United States.

While Campus Crusade for Christ has always been known for evangelism, they are equally committed to helping mature believers in their walk with Christ. Bill saw no dichotomy between evangelism and discipleship; he believed that true disciples are also soul winners. "If we're not fishing, we're not following," he often said (see Matthew 4:19). Here again, the founder's spiritual DNA is woven into the organization. In the early years of Campus Crusade, Bill authored *Ten Steps toward Spiritual Maturity* and a number of supplemental booklets called "transferrable concepts." His commitment to using the printed page for winning people to Christ and nurturing believers eventually culminated in yet another arm of ministry, Here's Life Publishers.

While Bill's overarching legacy is his contribution to the fulfilling of the Great Commission, several supporting themes he spotlighted helped spark entire movements. His life-long study of the attributes of God launched hundreds of thousands into their own ever-expanding walk with God. In 1994, God impressed Bill to mobilize prayer for revival and spiritual awakening in America. Bill's emphasis on prayer and the benefits of fasting gave tremendous impetus to the prayer movement in America. In fact, a focus on prayer is where Vonette found her niche in ministry. She helped found the National Prayer Committee and served for nine years as chair of the National Day of Prayer Task Force.

Of course, I cannot speak for Bill Bright. However, because Bill was so creative and innovative, I feel I'm on safe ground in believing he would have approved of the U.S. ministry's new, shortened name, Cru. According to the website, the reason for the name change is in keeping with the ministry's objective: "We want to do a better job of connecting people to God's love and forgiveness. It's all about helping people experience the good news that Jesus offers."[9] This is very much in the spirit of the founder.

In my lifetime, perhaps no one gave of himself more in promoting the cause and kingdom of Christ more than Bill Bright. He was prolific throughout his life as the visionary founder of Campus Crusade for Christ and as a prominent voice in several other ministries. When asked what energized him to accomplish so much Bill replied, "The filling of the Holy Spirit and the knowledge that the harvest is not forever. It soon will be past."[10]

Over the years Bill received many honors including honorary doctorate degrees from five schools, induction into the Oklahoma Hall of Fame, and the prestigious Templeton Prize for Progress in Religion in 1996. He donated the $1.1 million prize money to causes promoting the spiritual benefits of fasting and prayer.

Bill was a prolific writer, authoring over 100 books and pamphlets and numerous articles. Several of his books and pamphlets were translated into most major languages and distributed by the millions. His ministry through media continues today through the Bright Media Foundation.

In 1980, he courageously co-chaired with Pat Robertson the massive Washington for Jesus event. The purpose was to bring a wide range of Christians together to pray for America. Washington for Jesus was the first event to bring one million people together on the Capitol Mall. In addition to founding Campus Crusade for Christ International (CCCI), he was a major force in 1983 being proclaimed "The Year of the Bible" by President Ronald Reagan. One of his final projects was to co-found the Global Pastors Network and cast the vision of winning one billion people to Christ worldwide and planting five million new churches.

Neither age nor disease stopped him from his passion to see Christ exalted and the Great Commission fulfilled. As his body was increasingly ravaged with pulmonary fibrosis and he fought for every breath, he remained totally engaged in reaching people for Jesus Christ. Often he would literally go from the oxygen tank to the studio to capture one more session. Then it was back to the oxygen tank. During the last two years of his life, although much of the time he was confined to bed, he was involved in some 80 projects designed to bring people to faith in Christ and train them as His disciples.

In his final interview, given just a few weeks before his death, he reminisced, "The most important thing I ever did apart from my salvation, with my dear wife, Vonette, was to sign a contract to be slaves of Jesus. So all these more than 50 years we have sought to love Him with all of our hearts, all of our souls, all of our minds, and all of strength; to obey His commands and trust His promises."[11]

Bill Bright entered the presence of his Lord on July 19, 2003. Shortly before his death he wrote, "I respect all the profound theological propositions one can, and probably should, absorb; but right now, if it does not pertain plainly to life or death, heaven or hell, and the fulfillment of the Great Commission, my interest is short-lived."[12]

In reviewing his life, Dr. Bright observed, "Regrets? If I had my life to live over, I would have trusted Christ sooner and sought to have the faith to recruit and train more Spirit-filled followers of Jesus to help fulfill the Great Commission."[13]

"God has placed in our trust a measure of time, a unique set of talents, and sufficient resources to carry out His will for each of our lives," Bill said. "Our task as faithful stewards is to manage those blessings in order to bring maximum glory to His name."[14] How fitting that, at Bill Bright's gravesite, three words are written on his headstone: SLAVE FOR JESUS.

CHAPTER 3

Attempt Great Things

Missionary	William Carey
Birth	1761 in Northampton, England
Death	1834 in Serampore, India
Legacy	Known to many as the father of modern missions, William Carey awakened world missions interest in England through his preaching and the publication of his landmark study, *An Enquiry Into the Obligation of Christians to Use Means for the Conversion of the Heathens* in 1792. He completed translations of the Bible into Bengali, Sanskrit, and Marathi. Carey founded Serampore College to train pastors. After the loss of his manuscripts in a fire in 1812 he stood firm in his calling and began his work again. Carey introduced botany to India and fought against widow burning and infanticide. Even some Hindu scholars trace the roots of modern India to Carey. Numerous theological schools have been named in his honor. William Carey Library publishes and distributes missions books.
Quote	Expect great things from God; attempt great things for God.

I am a debtor both to Greeks and to barbarians, both to wise and to unwise. So, as much as is in me, I am ready to preach the gospel to you who are in Rome also. For I am not ashamed of the gospel of Christ, for it is the power of God to salvation for everyone who believes, for the Jew first and also for the Greek (Rom. 1:14–16).

The man who would later be called "the father of modern missions" was born in a humble home outside of Northampton,

England, in 1761. He had no unusual skills, no particular traits to indicate that he would shape the face of the Church for centuries. Yet he did just that. In fact, he probably did as much as anyone else in history to stir the imagination of Christians for world missions. How was he able to accomplish so much? "I can plod," Carey said. "I can persevere in any definite pursuit. To this I owe everything."

Carey was converted to Christ and became active in church while still a teenager. He took a job as a shoemaker when he was 16 years old, and when he was 24 he began to preach in a small Baptist church in the village of Moulton and teach in the village school. During these early years of ministry, God was working into Carey's heart a deep desire to reach the unevangelized.

William always had a book propped open at his cobbler's bench. He taught himself Greek, little knowing it would prepare him for his later ministry. By his own efforts he also learned Latin, Hebrew, Italian, Dutch, and French.

Carey married a childhood friend, Dorothy, and they had several sons. Their marriage, however, was not always a happy one. Dorothy suffered physical and emotional illnesses, though she and the boys followed Carey to India in his missionary undertakings.

In 1789, Carey accepted the pastorate of a large church in Leicester. His concern for those who had not heard the gospel grew, and in 1792 he published a small book that presented a powerful case for the church's involvement in missions. *An Enquiry Into the Obligation of Christians to Use Means for the Conversion of the Heathens* (this is the shortened title!) would eventually be ranked as one of the most important pieces of literature in Christian history. In the book, Carey wrote of Christ's Great Commission: "This commission was as extensive as possible, and laid [the disciples] under obligation to disperse themselves into every country of the habitable globe, and preach to all the inhabitants, without exception or limitation."

That same year, Carey preached a missions message to pastors in which he challenged them to "expect great things from God, attempt great things for God." In response to Carey's call, these ministers formed the Baptist Missionary Society.

Carey's zeal for world missions was not always appreciated. When he tried to encourage a group of Christians to reach the unreached, one man retorted, "Young man, sit down. When God pleases to

convert the heathen, He will do it without your aid or mine." But Carey would not be silenced, and his fire could not be put out. His passion for world missions had taken hold in his church. After the church released their pastor for India a member wrote, "For several years we have been praying for the spread of Christ's kingdom among the heathen; and now God requires us to make the first sacrifice to accomplish it."[1]

Carey sailed for India in 1793. Arriving in Bengal, he immediately set out to learn the language. Although Carey was disappointed that only a few were converted to Christ in his early days in Bengal, he persevered in his study of the Sanskrit language and completed a translation of the Bible into Bengali. Then he set up a press to print the new Bibles. During this time he also established schools and began medical care for the people of the area. In 1800, Carey moved with his family to the Danish colony of Serampore. He would spend the next 34 years in that part of India.

Through the years, Carey would face many personal and family hardships. One of his greatest trials occurred in 1812 when his priceless manuscripts were destroyed in a fire. A massive dictionary of several languages, two grammar books, and whole versions of the Bible went up in smoke. But Carey accepted the tragedy as the Lord's discipline and began again. "There are grave difficulties on every hand," he wrote, "and more looming ahead. Therefore, we must go forward."[2]

A list of what this one man accomplished over the years is staggering. Along with his pastoral duties and preaching, he translated the Scriptures in whole or in part into 37 languages. He produced complete translations of the Bible into Bengali, Sanskrit, and Marathi, and his stories in Bengali formed the basis for modern Bengali writing.

Carey founded the Serampore College for the training of Indian pastors and evangelists, as well as establishing churches. He founded the beautiful botanical gardens near Calcutta, for which he received the appreciation of all Asia. His influence also helped abolish *suttee*, the terrible practice of burning to death Hindu widows as part of the funeral service of their husbands, when the men's bodies were burned in a bonfire.

Even some non-Christian India scholars suggest that, long before Mohandas Gandhi, the true beginnings of modern India are traced to William Carey. William died in 1834. Rober Hall, a contemporary of William, paid tribute to him as "a man who unites with the most profound and varied attainments the fervor of an evangelist, the piety of a saint, and the simplicity of a child."[3] His impact is still felt across India and around the world.

CHAPTER 4

NO SCAR?

Missionary	Amy Carmichael
Birth	1867 in Millisle, County Down, Northern Ireland
Death	1951 in Tinnevelly, India
Legacy	Amy Carmichael courageously exposed what the *Sunday School Chronicle* called "a wickedness and degradation so colossal and so deep-seated" that few even attempted to intervene. Formed Dohnavur Fellowship in 1901 to rescue young girls forced into temple prostitution. The Dohnavur Fellowship eventually educated, cared for, and trained hundreds of children for lives of service. Known for her deep walk with Christ, she became a respected author whose books continue to have wide readership today. She influenced many to missionary service, including Jim Elliot and Elisabeth Elliot, who wrote a biography of her life.
Quote	Give me the love that leads the way, The faith that nothing can dismay, The hope no disappointments tire, The passion that will burn like fire. Let me not stoop to be a clod; Make me Thy fuel, Flame of God.

But Jesus said, "Let the little children come to Me, and do not forbid them; for of such is the kingdom of heaven" (Matt. 19:14).

As a young woman on the mission field in India, Amy Carmichael hiked alone to a cave in the mountain called Arima. "I had feelings of fear about the future. That was why I went there, to be alone with God. The devil kept on whispering, 'It's all right now, but what about afterward? You are going to be very lonely.' And he painted pictures of loneliness — I can see them still. And I turned to my God in a kind of desperation and said, 'Lord, what can I do? How can I go on to the end?' And He said, 'None of them that trust in Me shall be desolate.' That word has been with me ever since. It has been fulfilled to me. It will be fulfilled to you."[1]

Amy Carmichael committed her life to serve the Lord as a single woman amidst the uncertain circumstances of life on the mission field. Her love for and faith in Christ would challenge Christians in their commitment and trust for years to come.

Along with several other missionary women in India, Amy established the Sisters of Common Life, a spiritual order of single missionaries committed to exhibiting "Calvary love." This love is still seen today in the ongoing work of the Dohnavur Fellowship, which cares for children throughout India. Amy's 35 books and numerous poems are a lasting legacy that have stirred missions involvement worldwide.

Born December 16, 1867, in the village of Millisle on the north coast of Ireland, Amy was raised in a devout Christian home. Although Amy made a special commitment to trust the Lord in India, she witnessed God's protection and faithfulness years before she ever sailed for that country.

Amy's grandmother lived near the sea, where the tide is one of the strongest in the world. However, Amy and her brothers, Norman and Earnest, were permitted to go rowing within certain limits and were caught in a swift current.

"I was steering," Amy recalled. "My brothers were rowing hard, but they were powerless against the current. 'Sing!' they shouted to me, and I sang at the top of my voice the first thing that came into my head: 'He leadeth me, O blessed thought.' "

Strengthened by the words of the powerful hymn, the children were able to row the boat to safety.[2]

As a student in Ireland, Amy accepted the Lord Jesus as her Savior. Two years later, she had an experience that forever marked her values.

On a warm Sunday afternoon, Amy and her brothers were headed home from church. Suddenly, the three young people came upon a frail, elderly woman, bent over with a heavy bundle. Seeing her need, they offered to help the woman. Norman and Earnest lifted the load from the

> "No wound? No scar?
> Yet, as the Master shall the servant be,
> And pierced are the feet that follow Me;
> But thine are whole: can he have followed far
> Who had no wound nor scar?"
>
> ~ AMY CARMICHAEL ~

woman's arms, and Amy reached out to support her while she walked. Looking up, they noticed that several people from their church had stopped to stare. The scene was much like that in the story of the Good Samaritan, where the religious people passed by arrogantly while the Samaritan helped the robbed and beaten victim.

Later, when Amy remembered feeling the pain of the church people's self-righteous looks, she said, "I knew something had happened that changed life's values. Nothing could ever matter again but the things that were eternal."[3]

As a teenager, Amy went to care for Robert Wilson, the chairman of the famous Keswick Conventions (Bible conferences emphasizing a deeper relationship with God). Amy was drawn to these meetings because the teachings represented what she longed for in her life. Wilson's wife and daughter had died, so he loved Amy as his own daughter, and Amy cherished him, calling him the D.O.M. (Dear Old Man). When Amy was called to missionary service, the D.O.M.'s heart was torn, yet he knew he had to release Amy to God's will.

Her call to missionary service came clearly on January 13, 1892. Two words from the Lord, *Go ye*, were put deeply in her heart. Immediately, she made plans to serve the Lord as a missionary. For a time she served in Japan; then she went to India where she served for 55 years without a furlough.

Early in her missionary career, Amy learned a hard lesson. She went to visit an old lady who was ill. As Amy spoke through her translator to this Japanese woman, she seemed eager to open her heart to the Lord. Then something happened. The old woman noticed Amy's fur gloves and became disinterested in the message. "I went home," Amy reflected, "took off my English clothes, put on my Japanese Kimono, and never again, I trust, risked so very much for the sake of so little."[4]

In Japan, Amy also learned to battle the powers of darkness. A Buddhist neighbor was possessed by the "fox spirit," as the Japanese termed it. Amy assured the wife of the demon-possessed man that she and other missionaries would pray until he was delivered. Within an hour, a messenger came to say that all the "foxes," six of them, were gone. The next day, the man, perfectly well, came to Amy with a bouquet of flowers to express his appreciation. Some time later, he died peacefully, with his New Testament in his hands.

Settling in southern India, Amy served first with the Zenana Missionary Society of the Church of England. There she was associated with Thomas Walker, the famous missionary to Tinnevelly.

Amy's love for Christ led her naturally to respond to what she often referred to as "the Great Unrepealed Commission." For Amy, Christ's commission to us to disciple all nations remained in effect until the job got done or Christ Himself repealed His mandate.

In 1901, she formed the Dohnavur Fellowship with the purpose of rescuing children from the corruption of temple service. Often little girls were "married to the gods" during religious ceremonies and were forced to endure shameful abuse. Amy attempted to rescue these poor children and for years cried out against this social evil. Though the Indians knew this practice was one of the "secret sins" of Hinduism, many missionaries did not believe that such a horrible practice existed. Amy was often accused of kidnapping. The natives hated her, and the missionaries envied her. But she stayed at the task of rescuing these unfortunate children. By 1913, the Donavur Fellowship had housed and educated 130 children whose lives would have been a disaster without Amy.

Amy was also misunderstood for her insistence on "hearing the voice of the Lord" in matters pertaining to the Fellowship. Of course, Amy did not mean that she heard God's voice out loud. But she believed it was vital to hear Him on the inside and obey what was heard. She was able to "hear" God's voice because she stayed close to Him in prayer. Truly, Jesus was her dearest friend.

Amy left us the gift of her deeply spiritual writings — 35 books and poems.

CHAPTER 5

No Greater Love

Missionary	Jim Elliot
Birth	1927 in Portland, Oregon
Death	1956 in "Palm Beach," Ecuador
Legacy	After their martyrdom, *Life* magazine published a ten page article on the mission and death of Jim Elliot and his four missionary friends. Applications to mission agencies surged as hundreds of young people volunteered for service, inspired by Elliot's brief, courageous life. His wife, Elisabeth, along with others would establish a work among the feared Waodoni tribe which continues to this day. Elisabeth immortalized her husband's story in *Shadow of the Almighty* and *Through Gates of Splendor*. In 2006 the movie *End of the Spear* again brought attention to the bravery and love for Christ of these five young men. In Elliot's final letter to his parents he wrote, "I know you will pray. Our orders are 'the gospel to every creature.'"
Quote	He is no fool who gives what he cannot keep to gain what he cannot lose.

Greater love has no one than this, than to lay down one's life for his friends (John 15:13).

"God, I pray Thee, light these idle sticks of my life and may I burn up for Thee. Consume my life, my God, for it is Thine. I seek not a long life but a full one, like you, Lord Jesus."[1] God answered this prayer of Jim Elliott. He burned with zeal to take the gospel to the unreached peoples of South America. In a bold attempt to reach the indigenous Huaorani people, he laid down his life for Christ.

Jim Elliot committed to live for Christ at an early age. But it would have been difficult *not* to be a follower of Jesus Christ in the Elliot household. Living in Portland, Oregon, Jim's parents were a godly couple who made sure their home was always warm and inviting for friends, especially missionaries.

In high school, Jim was outspoken in his commitment to the Lord. He took the Bible seriously and literally. And some of the conclusions he drew made him unpopular with his classmates. Nevertheless, most of the students respected him, and they elected him president of his senior class.

Jim's interests in high school led him to develop skills that would later help him on the mission field. From what he learned about architecture, he helped build simple churches in Ecuador's jungles. And his interest in speech gave him the ability to share his faith in Christ.

After high school, Jim enrolled at Wheaton College, a Christian school in Illinois with a strong commitment to missions. He liked the school's motto because it fit his own: "For Christ and His kingdom."

Jim gained a new appreciation for his home and parents during this first separation, which was reflected in this letter:

> This is the spring of my nineteenth year. Slowly I have come to realize that my arrival at this point is not of my own efforts, not merely by the sure ticking of this winged racer Time, but by the quiet, unfelt guidance of a faithful mother and a father-preacher who has not spent so much time rearing other people's children that he hasn't had time for his own. . . . I am grateful to you and to our mutual Father, who has loved us all with a Love unknowable.[2]

While at Wheaton, Jim collected his thoughts in a diary, which was published after his death as a book called *Jim Elliot's Journal*. This journal contains some of the most deeply spiritual ideas recorded in the 20th century — and they were written by a college student.[3] Whether he sensed he would die young, we do not know.

We do know he lived with a sense of urgency. At age 21 he wrote in his journal, "How few, how short these hours my heart must beat — then on, into the real world where the unseen becomes important."[4]

While in college, Jim became even more interested in remote peoples not yet reached with the gospel. He was president of the Student Foreign Missions Fellowship. He gained physical strength as a champion wrestler and majored in New Testament Greek so he would be better equipped as a Bible translator. The degree he most desired, however, was what he termed the A.U.G. degree — Approved unto God.

> "He is no fool who gives what he cannot keep to gain what he cannot lose."
>
> ~ JIM ELLIOT ~

Jim knew that the kind of missions work he wanted to pursue was dangerous, for many of the tribes were truly savage. Yet Jim comforted himself in God's sovereign direction. He wrote his brother, encouraging him to boldly obey God's leading: "You are immortal until your work is finished."

Jim Elliot believed that the greatest qualification for effectiveness in Christian work was godly living. In his journal he wrote, "I see tonight that in spiritual work, if nowhere else, the character of the worker decides the quality of the work. . . . No wonder so much work in the Kingdom today is shoddy — look at the moral character of the worker."[5]

After graduation, he continued to prepare to be a missionary while awaiting approval from his local church. During this time, as God was focusing Jim's attention on the Quichuas, a vast indigenous community in South America, he wrote, "Consider the call from the throne above, 'Go ye,' and from round about, 'come over and help us,' and even the call from the damned souls below, 'Send Lazarus to my brothers, that they come not to this place.' Impelled, then, by these voices, I dare not stay home while Quichuas perish."[6]

Finally, the day he had prayed for came. On February 4, 1952, Jim Elliot departed by ship with Pete Fleming for Ecuador. Jim's parents were on the pier, weeping with joy as their son's ship sailed out of sight.

Jim launched into his work with youthful vigor. After several happy months in Quito, the capital, Jim went farther into the interior of Ecuador, to Shandia, a village at the base of the magnificent Andes mountain range. Earlier, at Wheaton, Jim had met a fellow student named Elisabeth Howard, who shared his deep spirituality and attraction to missions. Through the years since college, Jim and Elisabeth had allowed God to rule their romance and now their faith was rewarded. They were married in a simple service in Quito on October 8, 1953. This happy young missionary couple worked well as a team, ministering to the Quichuas. Their only child, Valerie, was born in February of 1955.

More and more, Jim pursued tribes who had not yet heard the gospel. He knew that God had promised that there would be people from every tribe among the redeemed. Around the throne, the redeemed would one day sing, "You . . . have redeemed us to God by Your blood out of every tribe and tongue and people and nation" (Rev. 5:9). Elliot wrote, "This is specific indication that the gospel must be gotten to tribes who are not yet included in the singing hosts. Hence, my burden for cultural groups as yet untouched."[7] For Elliot, this burden pointed in a clear direction — toward the Aucas.[8]

The Aucas were a feared, savage tribe who seemed straight out of the Stone Age. These isolated manhunters had successfully fought off any intrusion of civilization. They numbered in the thousands and were untouched by the good news of Jesus Christ. Few from the outside had ever entered Auca territory. Even fewer had come back.

Elliot and four other young missionaries decided it was their responsibility to reach the Aucas. "The prayer that had been in Jim's heart for years was prayed with renewed energy now — that those who still had never heard, who had never even had the chance to reject the gospel message, might hear. Many Quichuas had heard; many had rejected; but their blood was now upon their own hands. The blood of the Aucas, however, Jim saw on his own."[9]

Preliminary flights were made over Auca land. Gestures of friendship were made from the low-flying plane; gifts were dropped to the Aucas. Then it was time to go personally, to risk face-to-face encounters with the Aucas.

Before the trip, Jim and Elisabeth finished a translation of the Gospel of Luke for the Quichuas. They also talked frankly about the possibility that he might not return. Yet Jim believed the time was right.

The five brave missionaries penetrated Auca territory and made friendly contact with an Auca woman. Encouraged, the men radioed their wives to keep praying. But soon the transmissions went still, and communications ceased. On January 8, 1956, Jim Elliot and the four other missionaries were brutally murdered by those they had attempted to reach with God's message of love.

On the day of their martyrdom, the five missionaries to the Waodoni (including Jim Elliot) sang this hymn:

> We rest on Thee, our Shield and our Defender,
> We go not forth alone against the foe,
> Strong in Thy Strength, safe in Thy keeping tender,
> We rest in Thee, and in Thy name we go.
>
> Yea, in Thy name, O Captain of Salvation,
> In Thy blest name, all other names above,
> Jesus our Righteousness, our sure Foundation,
> Our Prince of Glory, and our King of Love.
>
> We go in faith, our own great weakness feeling,
> And needing more each day Thy grace to know,
> Yet from our hearts a song of triumph pealing,
> We rest in Thee, and in Thy name we go.
>
> We rest on Thee, our Shield and our Defender,
> Thine is the battle, Thine shall be the praise
> When passing through the gates of pearly splendor,
> Victors, we rest with Thee through endless days.[10]

The true heroes of this story are not only the men who laid down their lives for Christ, but also the brave wives and families who picked up the pieces of their shattered hopes and continued to serve the Lord. Elisabeth Elliot, with their young daughter, determined that now, more than ever, the Aucas must have the gospel. Along with the others, they lived among the Aucas, courageously forgiving the very men who had murdered their husband and father. Today, hundreds of Aucas are Christians. They are even sending some of their own people as missionaries to surrounding tribes.

When the news of the death of the five missionaries was announced in Christian schools, hundreds of young people volunteered to take their place. The story caused world mission to be front-page news in *Life* magazine and newspapers around the world. Elisabeth's books about Jim's death, *Through Gates of Splendor*, and his life, *Shadow of the Almighty*, became missionary classics. Thousands of people today are challenged by *The Journals of Jim Elliot*. ". . . he being dead still speaks" (Heb.11:4).

Elisabeth Elliot returned to live among the Huaorani along with a few other missionaries. Because of their courageous ministry among them, today many Hauorani are ardent followers of Jesus Christ, including Mincaye, one of the tribesmen who killed the missionaries. She became a prolific author, hosted a national radio program, and became a sought-after conference speaker. Valerie is married to a pastor.

Two films, *Beyond the Gates of Splendor* and *End of the Spear*, tell the stories of the gallant missionaries who laid down their lives advancing the gospel. And Jim Elliot, having surrendered what he could not keep, has gained what he could not lose.

CHAPTER 6

GIVE THE WINDS A MIGHTY VOICE

Mission Leader	Charles E. Fuller
Birth	1887 in Los Angeles, California
Death	1968 in Pasadena, California
Legacy	Charles E. Fuller was the most notable pioneer in using radio to spread the gospel. His weekly program, *The Old Fashioned Revival Hour*, aired from 1937 to 1968. For years the broadcast enjoyed one of the largest listening audiences of any radio program. It was carried by the Mutual Radio Network and later the ABC Radio Network. Airing live during the war years from the Municipal Auditorium in Long Beach, many servicemen came to faith in Christ through his compassionate preaching. Fuller founded the Gospel Broadcasting Association, the Fuller Evangelistic Association, and his enduring legacy, Fuller Theological Seminary (named for his father). The seminary's School of World Mission (now called the School of International Studies) has been a leader in training students worldwide for global evangelization.
Quote	My ambition is to see the world evangelized in this generation.

To the weak I became as weak, that I might win the weak. I have become all things to all men, that I might by all means save some. Now this I do for the gospel's sake, that I may be partaker of it with you (1 Cor. 9:22–23).

Charles E. Fuller wanted to use every available means "to get the gospel out" to as many people as possible, and the newest way

pel in Fuller's day was by radio. So he started the
evival Hour" radio program. And though he did
a missionary, Fuller's voice was heard around the
e message of Jesus.

The "Old Fashioned Revival Hour" drew larger audiences than any other program aired during radio's golden years of the 1940s. Twenty million people tuned in to the Sunday program, a larger audience than any Christian broadcast or telecast has today.

> "My ambition is to see the world evangelized in this generation."
>
> ~ CHARLES E. FULLER ~

Charles Fuller was born in Los Angeles to devout Christian parents. His father, who had been converted under the preaching of D. L. Moody, led his four sons in daily devotions, directing them in their relationships with the Lord.

Young Fuller excelled in athletics and academics. Captain of his college football team, he graduated with honors and later used his degree in chemistry to help manage his father's orange groves.

After college, Charles married his high school sweetheart, Grace Payton. "Honey," as he called her, later became the warm voice reading mail on the broadcast. In 1916, Charles Fuller attended a meeting conducted by evangelist Paul Rader because he wanted to hear what the former prizefighter had to say about Christianity. After the service, deeply moved by the Holy Spirit, Fuller drove his car to nearby Franklin Park in Hollywood. There he knelt on the floor of the back seat and gave his life to Christ. He later recalled:

> There had come a complete change into my life. Sunday, I went up to Los Angeles and heard Paul Rader preach. I never heard such a sermon in all my life. Ephesians 1:18. Now my whole life's aims and ambitions are changed. I feel now that I want to serve God if He can use me instead of making the goal of my life the making of money. I may have a call to go to the mission field in Africa.[1]

Both he and Grace entered the Bible Institute of Los Angeles (now Biola University) to prepare for Christian service. The godly dean of the institute, Dr. R. A. Torrey, told Fuller just before his graduation, "Young man, God has a great work for you."

Charles Fuller's popularity as a Bible teacher began to spread. He was ordained as a minister and pastored the Calvary Church in Placentia until 1933. Even in his early years of preaching, he stressed missions and evangelism.

Late one night, Charles Fuller awakened with thoughts of using radio to get the message of God's love to the people who might never go to church. At first, Fuller struggled with this call of God because he knew that it would be difficult to sustain a listening audience and maintain financial responsibility. His innovative use of radio to broadcast the good news was a bold step. He would later be called "the father of modern evangelism" because of his use of mass media to spread the gospel. Thus, he was the forerunner of a long stream of evangelists who later used television to bring God's message to the people.

However, Fuller obeyed God's directive, and throughout his life, he continued to try new ways to advance the message of Christ. He held large evangelistic rallies, helped sponsor 100 evangelists, founded a seminary with missions and evangelism as the heartthrob of the school, and carried on an international broadcast.

Before Billy Graham became a national evangelist, Charles Fuller conducted some of the largest evangelistic meetings in the country. Twice during his outdoor rallies, rain threatened to stop the meetings. On both occasions, the rain stopped immediately after Dr. Fuller prayed. In Chicago in 1946, with 68,000 people present, someone said the rain stopped as if someone "had turned off a faucet."

In the 1930s, during the Great Depression, times were hard for many American families. The Fullers, along with millions of others, had very little money. Their only son, Daniel, was seriously ill. Still, God gave the Fullers the promise from His Word that "great and mighty things" were in store for them.

Soon the broadcast Fuller had begun was picked up by other radio stations. He seemed to be touching a heartstring in America's soul. Through the brutal years of the Depression in the 1930s and

World War II in the 1940s, Charles Fuller and the "Old Fashioned Revival Hour" stood as a national symbol of hope and encouragement. During the war years, the Sunday afternoon service Fuller conducted from the Long Beach Municipal Auditorium was heard in many parts of the world. Ushers reserved 250 seats at the front of the auditorium for men and women in military service. Hundreds of young men who would later lose their lives in battle gave their hearts to Christ in those meetings. Fuller knew about this because he had asked Dawson Trotman, of the Navigators ministry, to help keep in touch with these new Christians.

In 1947, Charles expanded his international ministry by helping to found the Fuller Theological Seminary. Today the School of Intercultural Studies at Fuller Seminary trains Christian workers from many parts of the world.

Charles Fuller championed the little people, those in the "out-of-the-way places" — the shut-ins, the small farmers, the lonely soldiers. He reached them with the sincerity and compassion of his voice. His messages touched their hearts at their time of need.

Dr. Fuller's driving passion was to see people come to a saving knowledge of Jesus Christ: "My ambition is to see the world evangelized in this generation. I believe two things must be done before my responsibility has been fulfilled. First, to seek to be as effective as possible in preaching by radio; and second, to train others to preach."[2]

At the historic Congress on Evangelism in Berlin in 1966, evangelist Merv Rosell interviewed Fuller. Dr. Fuller gave excellent advice to young people seeking to serve Christ: "I would advise them first of all to let the Word of God dwell in them richly; that is master it. . . . Then it is so important to know the will of God, and that which you feel at home in and love to do. God will open the door."[3]

On March 18, 1968, Charles Fuller went home to heaven. His life was perhaps best summarized by Harold Ockenga, his long-time friend and co-founder of Fuller Seminary: "Here was a man of faith who took great risks for God."

CHAPTER 7

Before We Kill and Eat You

Missionary	H. B. Garlock
Birth	1897 outside of New Haven, Connecticut
Death	1985 in Dallas, TX
Legacy	H. B. Garlock experienced a notable missionary career with supernatural protection from cannibals, miraculous healings, and churches planted in Liberia, Ghana, and Malawi. Garlock was renowned as an expert on the continent of Africa and its peoples. He became the prototype of an effective Pentecostal missionary. His son, John, was for many years a popular professor at Christ for the Nations Institute. His ministry has been chronicled with the editorial and writing help of his daughter-in-law, Ruthanne, in *Before We Kill and Eat You*.
Quote	God was there protecting His servants. God had performed a miracle before our very eyes.

And He said to them, "Go into all the world and preach the gospel to every creature" (Mark 16:15).

H. B. Garlock was one of the last of the great wave of missionary pioneers to western Africa. Even though he lived in the 20th century, many of his missions adventures read like those of Paul in the Book of Acts.

The eldest of 12 children, Garlock was raised by God-fearing parents. He began to serve the Lord when he was a child, but at age 16, Christmas Day 1913, he had a powerful encounter with the Holy Spirit. Soon he determined to leave the family farm in Connecticut to go to Bible school.

His life was almost cut short by the influenza epidemic that swept the country immediately after World War I. While he was very ill, young Garlock received through a dream a clear call to missionary service. He knew God did not want his life to end; there was more for him to do. And soon, in answer to his parents' fervent prayers, he was on his feet again.

Within a few years of his narrow escape from death, Garlock was forging rivers, enduring famine and oppressive heat, and drinking the typhoid-infested water of untamed Africa. After completing his studies in 1920 at Beulah Height Bible School, H. B. and his sister Blanche determined to sail for Africa. Their parents accompanied them to the ship in New York harbor. They were presenting two children in one day for missionary service.

Liberia, in West Africa, was known as "the white man's grave," because so few missionaries survived the diseases and heat of the region. Also, cannibalism (the terrible practice of eating human flesh) was still practiced by many tribes. Into that difficult area, H. B. and Blanche Garlock settled as missionaries. When the first missionaries had rowed ashore only a few years earlier, an excited African ran to them and said, "I know who you are; you are missionaries! God appeared to me in a dream and told me to come to the coast and meet people who would preach good news to my tribe." Now the Christian message was gaining a foothold in a place bound by centuries of superstition.

In 1921, Garlock married Ruth Trotter, a girl he had fallen in love with in Bible college. They would serve the Lord together for many years, both in Africa and in the United States.

The Liberian people renamed Garlock, Kwi Kali, meaning "white bird." He started a church and opened a mission school in the village of Gropaka. King Jufuli, king of the region, sent his son to the mission school. There, young James heard amazing Bible stories for the first time. One morning, Garlock was reading the story of Jesus' healing blind Bartimaeus. James had cataracts, which caused him to be blind.

Upon hearing this Bible story, James asked if Jesus could make him see as He made Bartimaeus see. Garlock swallowed hard and told James to pray and believe. After a fervent prayer, the cataracts completely disappeared. The young man's face lit up, and he ran all the way into town to his father's house to show him what God had done.[1]

The people of Gropaka had asked for evidence of the power of the God the missionary preached. Now, here was living proof that Jesus was alive. The news spread rapidly, and many people put their faith in Jesus when they saw what had happened to James. King Jufuli renounced his worship of idols and gave his life to Christ, as did most of his counselors.

Garlock continued to see the miraculous power of God at work. Some time after the healing of Jufuli's son, H. B., along with several African helpers, trudged through thick jungle to rescue a young girl who had been kidnapped by another tribe. When he arrived at the tribe's village, he was surrounded by angry people with spears poised to attack. How would he escape? Garlock tells the story:

> They made a mad rush toward me with drawn knives, shouting, "Kill him, kill him!" The leader rushed at me with his cutlass raised to behead me. When it seemed the end had come and my head was about to be severed from my body, I closed my eyes and committed myself to God, repeating over and over again that one name that is above every name, "Jesus, Jesus!"
>
> Suddenly, there was a deathlike stillness! The tom-toms stopped beating and all screaming and yelling halted abruptly. . . . I cautiously opened my eyes — and wondered if I could believe them. Before me stood some of the savages with their weapons upraised ready to strike, while others held drawn knives by their sides. But all were frozen in their tracks. . . . The God that closed the lions' mouths in Daniel's time had held these wild, angry cannibals at bay!
>
> I have often wondered if they saw the Angel of the

Lord. . . . Or perhaps . . . they saw the horses and chariots of fire encircling our little company. One thing was certain — they did feel and see something that caused them to know that God was there protecting His servants. God had performed a miracle before our very eyes.[2]

A few years later, Garlock was again surrounded by an angry tribe of cannibals. The witch doctor threw his wand on the ground before Garlock as if to say, "Before we kill and eat you, you are permitted to speak." Garlock remembered Jesus' words in Mark 13:11: "Do not worry beforehand, or premeditate what you will speak. But whatever is given you in that hour, speak that; for it is not you who speak, but the Holy Spirit." He opened his mouth and a flood of words poured out that he had never learned. When he had finished, the witch doctor asked forgiveness on behalf of the tribe for trying to harm him. Again, the gospel had triumphed and Kwi Kali's life was spared.

As Garlock was making one of his frequent trips to preach to still another tribe, he saw a mountain that seemed strangely familiar to him. Yet he knew he had never been there before. Then he remembered. He *had* seen this mountain years before. When the Lord had called him to be a missionary when he was so ill with influenza as a teenager, He had shown him *this mountain* and assured the fever-ridden boy he would bring God's message to the people there. Now, years later, God fulfilled the promise.

Garlock would go to other missions works in Ghana and Malawi. He would pastor churches back in America in New Jersey, Colorado, and Kansas. In later years, he became the first field director for Africa for the Assemblies of God. But he would always remember that God spared his life so he could share God's love with even more people.

H. B. Garlock's daughter-in-law Ruthanne offered this assessment of his commitment: "H. B. Garlock would never be content to do a mundane day's work. His answer to God's call took him far beyond the comfortable and the ordinary, down paths where no line of retreat was kept open. He repeatedly placed himself in circumstances where God would have to reveal Himself in authority, or he would never leave the situation alive."[3]

CHAPTER 8

AMERICA'S FIRST MISSIONARY

Missionary	Adoniram Judson
Birth	1788 in Malden, Massachusetts
Death	1850 at sea in the Bay of Bengal
Legacy	Adoniram Judson was the first Protestant missionary sent from North America. His work in Burma led to the formation of the first Baptist association in the United States. Translated the Bible into Burmese, wrote A *Burmese Grammar* and was the primary researcher on the first Burmese-English dictionary. He planted several churches throughout Burma. Most evangelicals in Burma today trace their Christian roots to Judson. Judson University in Illinois is named after him, and in World War II the SS *Adoniram Judson* was named in his honor.
Quote	The prospects are as bright as the promises of God.

All authority has been given to Me in heaven and on earth. Go therefore and make disciples of all nations, baptizing them in the name of the Father and of the Son and of the Holy Spirit, teaching them to observe all things that I have commanded you; and lo, I am with you always, even to the end of the age (Matt. 28:18–20).

Few missionaries have ever had it tougher than Adoniram Judson. During his missionary service, he experienced the death of two wives and several children, battled frequent bouts of fever, and was brutally treated in a death prison for 17 months. In spite of all these sorrows, Judson still made one of the greatest impacts for Christ in history. In addition to his preaching ministry, Judson left the lasting treasures of several Bible revisions and translations and an English-Burmese dictionary.

Adoniram Judson was born in 1788 in Massachusetts, the son of a minister in the Congregational Church. Judson always excelled in school. When barely 16, he entered Brown College, graduating as valedictorian of his class after only three years.

Judson's inquiring mind caused him to ask hard questions about the Christian faith of his parents. At this time, he had not yet made a firm commitment to God. Nevertheless, after college he enrolled in the new Andover Theological Seminary.

Several events during this time brought Judson to a commitment to Christ. In a bizarre circumstance, while he was staying in a village inn, he heard the screams of a dying man in the room next to his. The next morning, he learned that the screams came from a close college friend who had died. This deeply affected Judson, and he began to seek answers about the Lord instead of asking more questions.

At Andover, he met Samuel Mills, who a few years earlier had spearheaded the famous "haystack prayer meeting" at Williams College. Some historians marked this unplanned outdoor prayer meeting as the true beginning of the missionary movement in America. While taking shelter from the rain under a haystack, several students pledged themselves to missionary service. They believed their commitment could spark the fulfillment of the Great Commission. "We can do it, if we will," they encouraged each other. Through his ongoing friendship with Judson, Mills was a key factor in pointing Judson to the mission fields of the world.

During his years of seminary, Judson dedicated his life to the Lord and to world missions. With Samuel Mills, Judson helped form the American Board of Commissioners for Foreign Missions. In 1812, Judson and his new wife, Nancy, boarded ship as the first American missionaries. They first disembarked in India, but circumstances pointed them toward Burma. Landing in Rangoon, they teamed with William Carey's son Felix to reach the Burmese with the gospel. They immediately set out to learn the difficult language, often studying 12 hours a day.

Judson and Nancy searched for new ways to reach the people.

They realized the Burmese did not respond well to church buildings like those in Western countries. They also observed that people thronged the local *zayats*, open areas for discussion and meditation. Between bouts of fever, the Judsons raised money and built a zayat for the purpose of sharing the gospel. Their plan worked, and soon there were several inquirers who became followers of Jesus Christ.

Their work was interrupted when war broke out between Burma and England. The Burmese government suspected all foreigners as spies and sentenced them all to prison. Judson's pleading that he was an American, not English, and had nothing to do with the military actions of England, fell on deaf ears, and he was sent to a Burmese death prison, a place for prisoners sentenced to die. Strung on bamboo poles for torture, the prisoners' feet and bodies were hoisted by pulleys until only their heads and shoulders remained on the floor. As the British advanced, the prisoners were driven northward. After over a year of no exercise and little nourishment, the march proved too much for many of the prisoners. Several died on the way. Although Judson survived the journey, he never fully recovered physically.

God used the Judsons to help preserve the Burmese Bible which Adoniram had painstakingly translated. This translation represented over ten years of agonizing work; there were no duplicates. If police found his work they would surely have destroyed it. To conceal the precious manuscript, his wife sewed its pages up in a pillow covered with cotton and rough cloth. She then paid the jailer to allow her to give this to Judson to help him sleep. Later, when the pillow was thrown in the trash by careless jailers, it was rescued miraculously by a Burmese Christian and returned to Mrs. Judson.

Sorrows continued to mount for Judson and his family. By 1826, Nancy and two of their children had died. In 1845, his second wife died. His work kept him away from home, and he experienced the agony of being separated often from his children.

Nevertheless, after a period of deep discouragement, new

> "The prospects are as bright as the promises of God."
>
> ~ ADONIRAM JUDSON ~

power from the Holy Spirit surged through Judson and he was refreshed to continue his preaching. In 1840, 28 years after landing in Burma, Judson completed his translation of the Burmese Bible and sent it to the press. Returning to America on furlough, he was afforded a hero's welcome. His name had become a household word among Christians. However, Judson was uncomfortable with this notoriety. He often disappointed his American audiences because he did not tell exciting missionary stories; instead, he preached the gospel.

While in America, he met and married Emily Chubbock, who returned with him to Burma. A gifted writer, she helped him complete a Burmese dictionary in 1849. Emily was expecting their second child when Judson became seriously ill. He left on a voyage, hoping to recover. But he died on the journey and was buried at sea.

Despite the illness and death of family members, Judson held to his faith in God. He never lost sight of his vision to evangelize Burma. As he stood against great odds, he was able to say, "The prospects are as bright as the promises of God."[1]

CHAPTER 9

THE FLYING SCOT

Missionary	Eric Liddell
Birth	1902 in Tianjin, China
Death	1945 in Weilhsien Interment Camp, China
Legacy	Eric Liddell was a devout Christian athlete who represented Great Britain in the 1924 Olympics, winning the gold medal in the 400 meters and the bronze medal in the 200 meters. Later as a missionary he taught at an Anglo-Chinese college. Interred along with other Westerners by the Japanese in World War II, his Christian character was known to all. He served in the camp as an arbitrator and pointed many to faith in Christ. In 2008 Chinese officials revealed that Liddell refused an opportunity to leave the camp, giving his place instead to a pregnant woman. He died of a brain tumor. His last words were, "It's complete surrender," referring to his relationship with God. Liddell's life is chronicled in the 1981 Academy Award-winning film, *Chariots of Fire*.
Quote	The secret in the 400m is that I run the first 200m as fast as I can. Then, for the last 200m, with God's help I run faster.

I press toward the goal for the prize of the upward call of God in Christ Jesus (Phil. 3:14).

Why would Hollywood be interested in making a film about a missionary from Scotland, 35 years after his death? Why did that film, *Chariots of Fire*, capture the hearts of millions and become the Academy Award-winning picture of the year? What is so special about Eric Liddell?

> "The secret in the 400m is that I run the first 200m as fast as I can. Then, for the last 200m, with God's help I run faster."
>
> ~ ERIC LIDDELL ~

Eric Liddell lived for Christ without compromise in the 20th century. Born of missionary parents in Tientsin, China, he later became the most popular and most widely known athlete Scotland had ever produced. A champion rugby player for Scotland's national team, he finally concentrated on his God-given ability to run.

Liddell's perseverance and commitment to Christ was evident throughout his athletic career. In an international contest in 1923, he was forced off the track as the runners scrambled for position in the 440-yard run. By the time he got up, the other runners were 20 yards ahead. With amazing determination, he caught up, then passed the other runners. He came in first and collapsed just across the finish line.

Liddell made world news in the 1924 Olympic Games in Paris. When it was announced that the heats of the 100 meters were to be held on Sunday, he refused to run. The Sabbath was to be devoted to the Lord, not to sports, Liddell said. Even those who did not agree with him admired this young man's unshakable convictions. Liddell chose to run the 400 meters instead, and even though he drew the outside lane, the hardest lane for that race, he won the race and the gold medal.

This world record holder was hailed as a national hero on his return to Scotland. He spent the next year as an effective evangelist, traveling throughout Britain and America. This world-famous man then quietly slipped out of the spotlight to pursue his life's call to China.

Affiliated with the London Missionary Society, he taught at the Anglo-Chinese College in Tientsin for a number of years. Then he accepted the hard challenge of rural evangelism, which often required many miles of travel by foot and bicycle under rugged conditions.

Liddell always showed compassion for the people to whom he ministered. After Japan's army occupied a province in China, Liddell helped to care for those wounded in the fighting. Several Chinese men were sentenced by the Japanese soldiers to be beheaded. One man refused to kneel to the swift swish of the soldiers' swords. The sword missed its mark, inflicting a deep gash from the back of the man's head to his mouth. He was left for dead. But Eric found the terribly wounded man and pulled him in a cart 18 miles to a mission hospital. Not only did the man live, but he became a follower of Jesus Christ.

Eric's athletic talents did not go unnoticed during his missionary career. Once, he was asked to run a race at an athletic meet in north China. He took it as an opportunity to testify to his faith in Jesus Christ. The crowd was so pleased at how he outdistanced the other runners that they persuaded him to run an extra race. What the crowd did not know was that Liddell's boat was due to leave in just a few minutes.

Having won the second race, Eric was about to leap into a waiting taxi when the playing of the national anthem forced him to stand at attention. He then jumped into the taxi, which sped across town, reaching the wharf just as the boat was moving out from the dock. A wave lifted the boat nearer to the dock, and Eric threw his bags on board, took a great leap, and landed on the departing boat!

Although Eric was devoted to getting the gospel to those who had not heard it, he also wanted to see Christians grow in their walk with the Lord. "The Christian life should be a life of growth," he said. "I believe the secret of growth is to develop the devotional life."[1]

Throughout his adult life, Eric kept an early morning time with God. He arose at 6:00 each morning to read Scripture and pray, giving emphasis to praying through the demands of the coming day and asking for God's guidance and strength.

In 1942, the Chinese province where Liddell served as a missionary was overrun by the invading Japanese. All foreign inhabitants, including missionaries and missionary children, were put in prison camps. Eric made the welfare of each prisoner his concern, even to the point of injuring his own health. He continued to preach Christ to the 1,800 people who were jammed into the camp, which measured only 150 by 200 yards. He encouraged the prisoners with his favorite Bible passages in 1 Corinthians 13 and Matthew 5, and he taught them to trust God through that ordeal with the words of a well-loved hymn:

> Be still, my soul: the Lord is on thy side;
> Bear patiently the cross of grief or pain;
> Leave to thy God to order and provide;
> In every change He faithful will remain.
> Be still, my soul: thy best, thy heavenly Friend
> Through thorny ways leads to a joyful end.[2]

Liddell became "Uncle Eric" to the missionary children, bolstering their courage by leading them in games. One man who survived the harsh camp as a child later said, "None of us will ever forget this man whose humble life combined muscular Christianity with radiant godliness. What was his secret? He unreservedly committed his life to Jesus Christ as Savior and Lord. That friendship meant everything to him."[3]

Eric wrote several books on Christian discipleship. In *Prayers for Daily Use*, published in 1942, he wrote about obedience as the key to developing intimacy with God: "Obedience to God's will is the secret of spiritual knowledge and insight. It is not willingness to know, but willingness to DO (obey) God's will that brings certainty."[4]

Liddell's wife, Florence, had been taken to safety in Canada. There she gave birth to their third daughter, whom Eric never saw.

Liddell died of a brain tumor in the prison camp shortly before he was to be released. A leading newspaper in Scotland wrote, "Scotland has lost a son who did her proud every hour of his life."

A fitting tribute was given at the end of *Chariots of Fire:*

> *Eric Liddell, missionary,*
> *Died in occupied China*
> *At the end of World War II.*
> *All of Scotland mourned.*

CHAPTER 10

THE STUDENTS' FRIEND

Mission Leader	Paul E. Little
Birth	1928 in Upper Darby, Pennsylvania
Death	1975 in an auto accident while vacationing in Canada
Legacy	Paul Little was a great advocate for evangelism, apologetics, and missions among college students. He served with InterVarsity Christian Fellowship and taught evangelism at Trinity Evangelical Divinity School. He provided strategic leadership for InterVarsity's Urbana Mission Conferences and the historic International Congress on World Evangelization in 1974 in Lausanne, Switzerland. He is best known for his practical, popular books, *Know Why You Believe* and *Know What You Believe*.
Quote	Witnessing is one of the keys to spiritual health. I like to call it the fizz in the Pepsi of the Christian life, because it puts sparkle and verve into our faith.

But in your hearts set apart Christ as Lord. Always be prepared to give an answer to everyone who asks you to give the reason for the hope that you have. But do this with gentleness and respect (1 Pet. 3:15; NIV).

Paul Little became a symbol for college students because of his joyful style of sharing his faith in Christ with others. Everywhere he went his message was received with enthusiasm, especially by America's Christian college students in the sixties and seventies. It seemed his life was cut short when, at the age of 46, on a well-deserved family vacation in Canada, he died in a traffic accident. But he is now more alive than ever as his ministry continues through his writings, recorded messages, and the people to whom he personally ministered during his life. He may now be reaching more people than ever before.

Paul Little was born December 30, 1928, to a devout Plymouth Brethren family in Upper Darby, Pennsylvania. The Plymouth Brethren have produced many famous Bible scholars, including H. A. Ironside and J. N. N. Darby. Because of the strong Christian influence in his home, it is no surprise that Paul became a Christian at an early age. Paul Little gave his heart to Christ on January 1, 1937, at the age of 8, but fully committed his life to Christ at age 13. Looking back, he said, "I knew the gospel from year one, through assembly meetings, Sunday school, and the reading of Scripture every day at home."

While still a teenager, Paul discovered that he had a heart condition that would probably prevent his entering the Christian ministry. So he determined to become a businessman. He enrolled in the Wharton School of Finance at the University of Pennsylvania, from which he received a bachelor of science degree.

While at Penn, he was active in the InterVarsity chapter, a group of Christian students meeting on his campus. When Little graduated in 1950, Joseph Bayle, a renowned Christian writer, asked Little to become an InterVarsity staff member. "It's one of the best things I ever did for the Christian witness in our universities and in the United States," Bayle said later.

Little was given an assignment for InterVarsity in New York City in 1953. There he met and began to date Marie Huttenlock, a former China Inland Missionary. She had been reassigned to minister to the 5,000 Chinese students who were stranded in New York as a result of the Korean War. Paul and Marie were later married.

Paul Little's ministry was wide and varied. He was always helpful to students, especially to those who struggled to know God's will for their lives. Students lauded his speaking style and sense of humor. Although Paul emphasized the importance of winning people to Christ, he also urged people to develop a growing devotional life. Addressing students at a missions conference, Paul said, "If you wait to *find* time, you will never find it. You have to *take* the time."

Little received a master of arts in biblical literature at Wheaton College and in 1964, became assistant professor of evangelism at Trinity Evangelical Divinity School. Since his death, the Paul Little Chair of Evangelism has been established at Trinity.

Little was a great crusader for foreign missions. His leadership in the Urbana Conventions and at the International Congress on World Evangelization in Lausanne, Switzerland, will always be remembered. Not only did Paul serve as assistant director and director of the Urbana gatherings, which are held every three years, but he was also a frequent speaker at the meetings. Little challenged thousands of students to consider foreign missions as their life work.

Billy Graham asked Paul Little if he would be the assistant program director for the International Congress for World Evangelization in 1974. After praying about it, Little accepted. He became very excited about this gathering of international church leaders, and he encouraged the participants to keep their eyes on the single great task of reaching the world with the gospel: "The tide is in for . . . witness around the world and the (feeling) was we should move on that tide toward the goal of world evangelization in this century."

Perhaps his most lasting contribution is contained in his writings. He authored three books: *How to Give Away Your Faith, Know Why You Believe,* and *Know What You Believe.* He also wrote several booklets and articles.

Paul Little set a tone for a style of evangelism that was both gracious and straightforward. In *How to Give Away Your Faith,* he urged Christians to be involved with non-Christians without compromising their Christian faith. He defended the truth that Jesus Christ is the only way to God, and only through Him can we have forgiveness of sins.

Little wrote an article only a few months before his death titled,

"The God Who Never Lets Things Just Happen." In it he wrote, "The apostle Paul wasn't looking to death as a cop-out, but rather as a fulfillment of the ministry God had given him. He had confidence in God for the future, whatever it might be. Your future and mine are uncertain, too . . . nothing happens by accident, and we can rest with confidence in that."[1]

CHAPTER 11

THE SMOKE OF A THOUSAND VILLAGES

Missionary	David Livingstone
Birth	1813 in Blantyre, Scotland
Death	1873 near Lake Bangweulu, Rhodesia
Legacy	David Livingstone, the most famous missionary of his time, was also a cartographer, explorer, and vocal opponent of the African slave trade. His influence fostered many mission schools across Africa which, in turn, graduated Africans who were at the forefront of national independence movements. He championed the cause of the evangelization of the African interior. Livingstone's motto, inscribed in the base of the statue to him at Victoria Falls, was, "Christianity, Commerce, and Civilization." His published journals became best-sellers, introducing many readers to the plights and potentials of Africa. There are numerous honors and memorials to his life. He is buried in honor among British royalty and other notables in Westminster Abbey.
Quote	I am a missionary, heart and soul. God had an only Son, and He was a missionary and a physician. A poor, poor imitation I am, or wish to be. In this service I hope to live; in it I wish to die.

But He said to them, "Let us go into the next towns, that I may preach there also, because for this purpose I have come forth" (Mark 1:38).

"God had an only Son and He made Him a missionary." These words, attributed to David Livingstone, revealed his passion for missions. Although Livingstone was an explorer, doctor, author, and cartographer (a person who charts maps), his enduring fame is as a missionary. In fact, David Livingstone is probably the most famous missionary of all time.

Born in humble surroundings in Blantyre, Scotland, in 1813, by the age of ten he was working up to ten hours a day in the textile mills. With his first earnings, he bought a Latin grammar book. Even though his education was sometimes hampered because he had to work, Livingstone had a thirst for knowledge. He took night courses and read medical journals and his Bible by the dim lights in the mills. He eventually received a degree in medicine and theology from Anderson's College, a part of Glasgow University.

Brought up in a strict Calvinistic faith, David joined an independent Christian congregation of even stricter discipline when he was 17. When he was 21, an appeal by British and American churches for qualified medical missionaries in China made him determined to become one. Then one night he heard a missionary challenge by the famous missionary Robert Moffat, who would one day become his father-in-law. Moffat, who had served along the coastline of southern Africa, challenged his audience to share God's love in "the vast plain to the north" where he had "sometimes seen, in the morning sun, the smoke of a thousand villages, where no missionary had ever been."[1]

Livingstone later recalled, "I saw the duty and inestimable privilege *immediately* to accept salvation by Christ. Humbly believing that through sovereign mercy and grace I have been enabled to do so . . . it is my desire to show my attachment to the cause of Him who died for me by devoting my life to His service."[2]

In 1840, Livingstone was ordained as a missionary, and the next year set sail for Africa to meet his destiny as a dedicated Christian, a courageous explorer, and a fervent anti-slavery advocate. Livingstone met with his family the night before he sailed for Africa. Together they read Psalm 121, noting the assurance, "The Lord shall preserve you from all evil; He . . . shall preserve your going out and your coming in" (v. 7–8). The next morning David's father walked him to the Liverpool steamer. They would never meet again.

Arriving in South Africa, he pushed his search for converts into northern territory where no white man had ever been. Trying to establish a mission station, he was mauled by a lion and suffered intense injury to his arm. Another accident made the injury worse, so he could never again support the barrel of a gun with his left hand.

Livingstone experienced many other adventures. He was the first white man to see Lake Ngami and the magnificent waterfalls of the Zambezi River, which he named after his queen, Victoria Falls. He hoped that the Zambezi, which he called "God's highway into the interior," could be navigated. Livingstone had witnessed the horrors of uncaring merchants capturing and selling Africans. Perhaps navigation of the Zambezi would result in a combination of "commerce and Christianity" which would end the ugly slave trafficking.

In 1845, Livingstone married Robert Moffat's daughter, and she accompanied him on many of his journeys. Her health and the need to provide security and education for their four children finally made it necessary for them to go home to England.

When Livingstone returned to England in 1856 after 16 years in Africa, he received a hero's welcome. While there, he wrote *Missionary Travels and Researches in South Africa*, which became an instant best seller, earning him even more fame throughout the civilized world. The next year, he made an impassioned plea to the young men of Cambridge University to join the missionary movement, especially in Africa. As a result, the Church Missionary Union at Cambridge was formed.

Livingstone returned to Africa to continue his explorations and his evangelistic work. In 1865, after another speaking trip through Britain on behalf of missions, he returned to Africa for the last time. When he disappeared into the heart of the continent, he did not see another European for almost seven years. Rumors spread that Livingstone had been captured or that he had died. In 1871, a famous American newspaper, the *New York Herald*, commissioned H. M. Stanley to go to Africa to find Livingstone.

An amazing set of circumstances eventually brought Stanley and Livingstone face to face in the thick of the African jungle. As they stared at each other, Stanley broke the silence with the now-famous words, "Dr. Livingstone, I presume."

During the next few days, Stanley urged the ill and aging Liv-

> **"I am a missionary, heart and soul. God had an only Son, and He was a missionary and a physician. A poor, poor imitation I am, or wish to be. In this service I hope to live; in it I wish to die."**
>
> ~ DAVID LIVINGSTONE ~

ingstone to return home with him. Stanley reminded him that he was world-famous, that his books were now classics, and that he could receive medical treatments for his diseases.

Livingstone declined. He had made a commitment to the Lord to both live and die in Africa. Weary, yet still committed to his task, he wrote these words in his journal: "My Jesus, my king, my life, my all. Once more I dedicate my whole self to Thee."

On May 1, 1873, the African helpers found David Livingstone dead, kneeling by his bed in a posture of prayer. Before his death, Livingstone had instructed his helpers to remove his heart from his body and bury it in Africa. His remains were then sent back to England where he was buried in honor alongside Britain's royalty and most prominent people in Westminster Abbey. Engraved on his burial marker is John 15:13: "Greater love hath no man than this, that a man lay down his life for his friends" (KJV).

Someone has said that not only did David Livingstone discover Africa, he discovered the African. His reports on the evil of slavery helped make it illegal throughout the civilized world. Throughout his time in Africa he promoted a combination of "commerce and Christianity." He believed healthy trade with the rest of the world and the spread of the gospel would lift Africa to realize its potential.

Today, Livingstone's passion for those who had not heard the gospel challenges a new generation of missionary pioneers. In keeping with the compassion of Livingstone, "the smoke from a thousand villages" drives them on.

CHAPTER 12

A CHRISTMAS GIFT FOR JESUS

Missionary	Lottie Moon
Birth	1840 in Albemarie County, Virginia
Death	1912 in Kobe Harbor, Japan
Legacy	Lottie Moon was a legendary Baptist missionary to China. An early proponent of cultural sensitivity, she adopted many Chinese customs. Her respect for what was beautiful in Chinese culture helped open the hearts of many Chinese to the gospel. She was an early proponent of regular furloughs for missionaries to increase longevity and fruitfulness. Her suggestion that a Christmas offering for missions be received in all Baptist churches has developed into the Lottie Moon Christmas Offering for Missions which has raised over $1.5 billion for mission outreaches worldwide. She has come to personify the missionary spirit of Southern Baptists.
Quote	How many there are . . . who imagine that because Jesus paid it all, they need pay nothing, forgetting that the prime objective of their salvation was that they should follow in the footsteps of Jesus Christ in bringing back a lost world to God.

How then shall they call on Him in whom they have not believed? And how shall they believe in Him of whom they have not heard? And how shall they hear without a preacher? And how shall they preach unless they are sent? (Rom. 10:14–15).

If one word were used to describe Lottie Moon, it might well be *courage.* As a single woman, she overcame great obstacles to bring the message of Christ to the people of north China. During her lifetime, her writings were a strong influence for missions in women's prayer groups in America. But the impact of her life has been far greater since her death.

Lottie was raised in a strong Christian home with the benefits of a good education. One night during college, a campus revival meeting brought her to total commitment to Christ. "I went to the service to scoff," she recalled, "and returned to my room to pray all night."[1]

Her sister Edmonia was one of the first two single women missionaries to be commissioned by the Southern Baptist Convention. But Lottie Moon would be the name that would be endeared to missions-minded Christians for years to come. After college, Lottie helped run the plantation where she was raised, and then became a school teacher in Georgia. But in her heart she longed to become a missionary. Because her other sisters had served as doctors, business executives, and even in military operations, Lottie did not believe that being a woman would hinder her effectiveness as a missionary. She was right. In 1873, one year after her sister Edmonia, Lottie Moon sailed for China.

> "How many there are . . . who imagine that because Jesus paid it all, they need pay nothing, forgetting that the prime objective of their salvation was that they should follow in the footsteps of Jesus Christ in bringing back a lost world to God."
>
> ~ Lottie Moon ~

Lottie's missionary commitment always came first. An old boyfriend, who was by then a professor, had proposed to her. Although Lottie had strong feelings for him, she could not endorse his belief in evolution. This disagreement was serious enough for Lottie to refuse his marriage proposal. Years later, Lottie was asked if she ever considered marriage. "Yes," she said, "but God had first claim on my life, and since the two conflicted, there could be no question about the result."[2]

In many ways, Lottie was ahead of her time. She insisted that women should have the same privileges and responsibilities as men in missions work. Believing it was God's will, Lottie established a church in the section of north China where she had been stationed. Lottie was also ahead of her time in her belief that the new church be "as free from foreign interference as possible." Over the next two decades, the church Lottie had started saw over a thousand people come to Christ and be baptized. Lottie wrote back excitedly to Christian women in America, "Surely there can be no deeper joy than that of saving souls."[3]

Indeed, her letters addressed to Baptist women in America's southern states became a powerful tool for missions. She urged the women to become involved in missions through their prayers and gifts. These fervent written pleas for the world's masses without Christ became the prayer focus of Baptist Women's Missionary Unions across the South. And while Lottie addressed her letters to Christian women, she sometimes chided men for their lack of concern. "It is odd," she wrote, "that a million Baptists of the South can furnish only three men for all of China. . . . I wonder how these things look in heaven. They certainly look very [strange] in China."[4]

Although she experienced some successes, Lottie was often frustrated in her attempts to win the Chinese to Christ. She sometimes found it difficult to identify with and communicate to the Chinese. However, she acted on one idea that has helped send out thousands of missionaries and has brought thousands more to faith in Christ. Lottie proposed a week of prayer for foreign missions and a special Christmas missions offering throughout Southern Baptist churches. The proposal was accepted, and since her death, the Lottie Moon Christmas Offering has brought in hundreds of millions of dollars yearly for missions.

After the Boxer rebellion in China in 1900, Lottie worked tirelessly to minister to the victims of the conflict. Plagues, smallpox, famine, and local fighting brought mass starvation to the Tengchow area where Lottie worked, and she drained her life's savings attempting to help the Chinese. Her health weakened and friends urged her to return to the States for medical treatment. She died on a ship returning to America on Christmas Eve 1912, one week after her 72nd birthday.

Today, Lottie Moon is the most famous Southern Baptist missionary, and her memory continues to stir the hearts of Christians to give through the Christmas offering for the advance of the gospel. People cannot go as missionaries unless they are sent by the prayers and giving of concerned Christians. Lottie Moon, without knowing it, has been responsible for sending out thousands of missionaries around the world.

CHAPTER 13

CHRIST'S AMBASSADOR

Mission Leader	John R. Mott
Birth	1865 in Livingston Manor, New York
Death	1955 in Orlando, Florida
Legacy	John R. Mott was the highly respected leader of the YMCA and World Student Christian Federation. Considered by many the greatest missionary statesman of the twentieth century, he presided over the 1910 World Missionary Conference in Edinburgh, the first truly international world mission conference. His visionary leadership helped propel the Student Volunteer Movement to send thousands of young missionaries. A prolific author, he is best known for *World Evangelization in This Generation*, which helped popularize the slogan of the Student Volunteer Movement. His advocacy for multiple Christian causes raised hundreds of millions of dollars. Mott received the Nobel Peace Prize in 1946 for his work in international church and missionary movements. He is interred in the National Cathedral in Washington, D.C.
Quote	In view of the constraining memories of the cross of Christ and the love wherewith He has loved us, let us rise and resolve, at whatever cost of self-denial, that live or die, we shall live or die for the evangelization of the world in our day.

That they all may be as one, as You, Father, are in Me, and I in You; that they also may be one in Us, that the world, may believe that You sent Me (John 17:21).

John R. Mott had been called "the most influential religious leader of the 20th century." His influence was perhaps even more widespread than that of his hero, David Livingstone. From the time he was a young person, Mott said, "I have never been disappointed." To many in our time, however, John R. Mott is largely forgotten. Who was he? Why was he such a force for missions?

John R. Mott was born in New York and raised in Iowa by God-fearing parents. He learned the message of the gospel in his Methodist home at a family altar. Later, as a college student at Cornell, he committed his life to Christ under the preaching of J. E. K. Studd, brother of the famous missionary C. T. Studd. One night, Mott slipped into a meeting just in time to hear Studd issue the challenge, "Young man, seekest thou great things for thyself? Seek them not! Seek ye first the kingdom of God." Mott took the challenge personally and from that time gave himself to the cause of Christ.

In 1886, he represented his college at the Christian Student Conference at Mount Hermon, sponsored by D. L. Moody. There, along with 100 other students, he signed the "Princeton Pledge," which stated, "I purpose, God willing, to become a foreign missionary."

Soon Mott was actively engaged in Christian endeavors. In 1888, he became the general secretary of the Student YMCA, which, at that time, gave priority to winning young men to faith in Christ. That same year, at the age of 23, he became the chairman of the Student Volunteer Movement (SVM) for Foreign Missions. Over the years he would be the driving force behind the SVM, which sent some 20,000 young people into the missionary ranks. Their rallying cry was "the evangelization of the world in this generation."

Mott explained his concept of missions this way:

> It is not necessary that we go to the Scriptures, or to the ends of the earth, to

> **"In view of the constraining memories of the Cross of Christ and the love wherewith He has loved us, let us rise and resolve, at whatever cost of self-denial, that live or die, we shall live or die for the evangelization of the world in our day."**
>
> ~ JOHN R. MOTT ~

discover our obligation to the unevangelized. A knowledge of our own hearts should be sufficient to make plain our duty. We know our need of Christ. How unreasonable, therefore, for us to assume that the nation living in sin and wretchedness and bondage can do without Him whom we so much need even in the most favored Christian lands.[1]

Mott was decades ahead of his time in missions strategy, championing the developing of national leadership. In 1901 he wrote, "Experience teaches that natives have been the chief human factor in the evangelization of different countries. No extensive field has ever been thoroughly evangelized but by its own sons. This seems to be God's method."[2] He believed in "the presentation of the living Christ to all men, and doing so in a way among each people or in each nation as will result in . . . naturalizing or making truly indigenous pure Christianity among them."[3]

The highlight of Mott's remarkable career as a voice for missions came in 1910 when he helped convene and preside over the World Missionary Conference at Edinburgh, Scotland. This conference, with 1,355 delegates, was the first inter-church conference on missions in modern times.

Mott was a man of great personal discipline. His life was anchored in a daily time of communion with God in prayer and Bible reading he called the Morning Watch. He saw this particular discipline as the single greatest asset to personal spiritual development.

He was ardently evangelistic, urging Christians to be vocal about their faith. He said, "The pervading purpose of the Christian church and of every other agency concerned with the spread of the Kingdom of God should be that of leading people to commit their lives to Christ as their Savior and Lord."[4] He also contended that one's devotion to Christ should permeate all of life. Mott said, "The governing purpose of the Church in the world is to make Jesus Christ known, trusted, loved, obeyed, and exemplified in the whole range of individual life and in all human relationships."[5]

John R. Mott modeled missionary statesmanship. He was full of vision, had great speaking skills, and was guided by eternal principles set forth in Scripture. Basil Matthews, who wrote one of two biographies on his life, saw Mott as "a man with a great idea incessantly at work on a world scale. . . . [Mott] has dedicated and disciplined every power of body, mind, and spirit to the incessant battle across the world, through decade after decade, for the Kingdom of God."[6]

Throughout his life, Mott continued to be a major voice for missions. He was also a prolific fund-raiser, garnering millions of dollars for Christian projects around the world. He always challenged young people to take Christ's message to the whole world. "The worldwide proclamation of the gospel awaits accomplishment by a generation which shall have the obedience, courage, and determination to attempt the task," he said.[7]

He was chairman of several influential missionary councils, including the International Missionary Council and the Conference of Missionaries to Muslims in 1928. Then in 1948 he was named co-president of the newly formed World Council of Churches. Mott was a pioneer in helping to bring together churches and denominations.

Mott worked tirelessly for unity and cooperation among Christians. He believed a united Christian witness was vital for effective evangelism and missions. Although he remained a Methodist layman, his wise council was sought by church leaders, presidents, and government officials worldwide. In 1946, he was awarded the Nobel Peace Prize for his work in reconciling individuals, churches, and nations.

Although he traveled tirelessly, Mott was a devoted family man. Leila, his wife for 62 years, often traveled with him, challenging young women to become missionaries, and ministering to missionary wives.

A few days before his death, Mott sent this message to the World Alliance of YMCAs, an organization he was strategic in building: "Old things are passing away. All things may become new. Not by magic nor by wishful thinking, but by self-sacrifice and the will to bring them about in the name of Jesus Christ."[8]

On January 31, 1955, John R. Mott died, passing his torch of world evangelization to others. Although he was the friend of kings and presidents, he viewed himself first as a soul winner. "While life lasts," Mott said, "I am an evangelist."[9]

CHAPTER 14

FROM ONE BROKEN HEART

Mission Leader	Bob Pierce
Birth	1914 in Fort Dodge, Iowa
Death	1978 in Los Angeles, California
Legacy	Bob Pierce founded two of the largest, most notable Christian organizations, World Vision and Samaritan's Purse. Known for both his volatility and great compassion, in his early ministry Pierce was an evangelist with the fledgling Youth for Christ ministry. A trip to Asia shortly after World War II galvanized his vision for both evangelism and relief aid offered in the name of Christ. His moving advocacy for humanity's disadvantaged helped American evangelicals gain a more holistic understanding of their world mission. Franklin Graham became his protégé and the second president of Samaritan's Purse.
Quote	Let my heart be broken by the things that break the heart of God.

For the love of Christ compels us, because we judge thus: that if One died for all, then all died; and He died for all, that those who live should live no longer for themselves, but for Him who died for them and rose again (2 Cor. 5:14–15).

Bob Pierce witnessed firsthand the horrors of the Korean War's effects on Korea's children. Deeply moved, he wrote in his Bible, "Let my heart be broken by the things that break the heart of God."

Little did Bob Pierce know the great cost that would be involved in the fulfillment of that prayer. But he did know that indelibly etched on his mind were the effects of the Korean War, where he had seen unclaimed children eating out of trash cans and sleeping under cardboard. Bob himself would suffer tremendous heartache — several illnesses, wrenching disagreements with friends, and the tragic loss of one of his daughters. But his commitment to helping others in pain led him to establish two great Christian caring ministries: World Vision and Samaritan's Purse. They were born, as one friend said, not so much as organizations but as the spurting blood from Pierce's broken heart.

Bob Pierce was born in Iowa in 1914. His godly parents encouraged him from birth to serve the Lord and lead a holy life. So it is not surprising that Bob came to Christ as a child. He was called to preach the gospel when he was 12. Bob's father died that same year. Through the grief, Bob remained committed to Christ, even though he stumbled along the way. He later recalled, "From that time at age 12, I've sinned, I've quit, I've failed, I've stumbled, I've fallen, I've landed in the mud puddle and come out drenched with mud. But one thing has been true: God set me apart and there's no way that I could run away from God. I have tried."[1]

After a time of study at Pasadena Nazarene College, he was ordained to the ministry. Soon afterward he met Lorraine Johnson, the daughter of a noted pastor in the Nazarene church. Bob and Lorraine were married and three daughters were born from this union. Their life was often hard and filled with many goodbyes, as Bob was off for another missionary journey. But the sacrifices of the Pierce family brought rich rewards to people around the world.

Bob was on the ground floor of the Youth for Christ ministry to Asia while Billy Graham opened YFC in Britain. Bob was involved with the movement because of its strong emphasis on winning young people to Christ.

While Bob Pierce is most remembered for his Christian philanthropy, his greatest motivation was to reach people with the gospel and bring them to faith in Christ. "I never wanted to be a famous anything. The passion of my soul since the day God called me . . . the *one thing* — has been that I wanted to see people come to the experience of being born again."[2] Bob knew that would be costly. His prayer in Korea for a broken heart was certainly answered. On his trip for Youth for Christ to the Orient, he felt he had to do something to relieve the suffering he saw everywhere, especially among the precious children. Of this time he later reflected, "The only measurement . . . I had in assessing what we should be in was, *Is this something Jesus would do? Something God would want done?*"[3]

Returning to the States, he launched a ministry dedicated to meeting emergency needs in crisis areas. The first project would be to sponsor the needs for education and basic care for thousands of Korean children. The result was World Vision. Today, this ministry is one of the largest Christian organizations in the world, helping needy people around the world in the name of Christ.

As founder and president of World Vision, Bob established an international relief program to help hungry, desperate children. As his heart had always gone out to pastors in other countries, he established conferences for these brave national church leaders. He organized tours for the Korean Orphans Choir, who sang their way into the hearts of thousands of Americans.

Those who knew Bob Pierce well often spoke of his unusual prayer life. He was constantly, earnestly praying. Much of the time he lived on the edge of a need for a miracle because his huge heart of compassion committed him and his organization to send money that simply was not available. Time after time, he responded to emergency needs of missionaries, then his prayer and faith went to work. He lived in what he called "God room," that area of faith where man's best efforts could not possibly resolve the situation. When the miracles came, only God could get the credit.

One of the first crossroads of faith he faced was when he obeyed God's leading for his initial visit to China. Not having enough money to buy a ticket to China, he went to the airport and purchased a ticket to Honolulu. Then he made a phone call to a friend. When the friend found out that Bob was on his way to Hawaii and was trusting God to provide the needed money to China, he offered to help raise funds for the rest of the trip and to wire the money to him in Honolulu. Bob had made that all-important first

> **"Let my heart be broken by the things that break the heart of God."**
>
> ~ Bob Pierce ~

step of obedience, and the rest of his needs were met.

Bob traveled the world over, giving hope to the discouraged — and many times the most discouraged were missionaries.

He served much time in Taiwan and Korea, and ministered to the American military in Vietnam. His radio broadcasts from the field to donors in America were some of the finest missionary broadcasts ever produced. Many people found that they read his letters of appeal through eyes blurred with tears. Bob, always a pioneer, also helped begin Great Commission Films, one of the first major Christian film ministries.

Bob Pierce drove himself for the Great Commission. He often worked himself past the point of physical and emotional exhaustion. Someone said he seemed to absorb all the pain he saw into his own body. Yet, even in his weakened condition, he remained true to the Lord and His calling. "The secret of lasting success," Bob often said, "is lasting!"

Although it took a great toll on him personally, Bob had an amazing ability to absorb the suffering of others. "I literally felt the child's blindness, the mother's grief," he said. "And there was no way that I could walk among the lepers and not feel as lonely, as cut off, as abandoned, as heartbroken, as debased and humiliated as they were. . . . And this is, I believe, one of God's gifts to me . . . I feel."[4]

After a conflict within the organization, Bob resigned as president of World Vision in 1967. Then, having regained a measure of his health, Bob formed Samaritan's Purse, a smaller ministry dedicated to ministering quickly to crisis situations.

Recognized as a Christian ambassador all over the world, he often was received by heads of state. Nevertheless, he longed for young Christians to see their high calling, saying, "We need men and women . . . who are humble before God, who are aware that their power comes from His indwelling Holy Spirit, and who are confirmed in their minds that God has given them a high calling as His ambassadors. Paul never hung his head before any king but King Jesus."

One of Bob's young "projects" was Franklin Graham, son of evangelist Billy Graham. Today, Franklin is the president of Samaritan's Purse.

Bob Pierce believed in a God of miracles. Once, in Korea, a man tried to disrupt an outdoor meeting where Bob was preaching, by parking a train locomotive close to the meeting and pulling the shrieking whistle every two or three minutes. Bob's response was dramatic. He stood before the audience and challenged the devil:

> I command you, Satan, in the name of Jesus Christ, to still that shrieking whistle and to get that man and his engine out of here at once, so that people who have never heard the gospel will hear and be saved. And I thank You, Lord, for defeating Satan, and I ask You in the name of Christ to command these demons and whoever they are who have brought this engine and disrupted this meeting to move it out of here and still that thing this very second.[5]

Immediately, the wheels of the train began to move and it backed off, out of sight and sound.

In the mid-1970s, Bob discovered that leukemia was rapidly invading his body. Even then, he did not lessen his pace. In fact, it seemed that he picked up his pace of meeting needs and preaching the gospel. During that time, someone remarked, "Have you heard that Bob Pierce is dying with leukemia?"

The friend replied, "No, he's not. He's *living* with leukemia."

Bob Pierce received numerous awards for his life of service. Three times he was decorated by the Korean government with the highest honor that can be given to a foreigner. He received honorary doctorates from Northwestern School in Minnesota, Yonsei University in Korea, and John Brown University in Arkansas. Yet his greatest reward is in heaven. Many thousands will be there because his love brought them to Jesus.

Bob involved himself in human need wherever he found it. He especially loved helping missionaries, whom he often referred to as heroes of the cross. "I'm not a missionary," he said, "but I own stock in half a dozen projects of one kind or another overseas."

He constantly challenged missionaries and national pastors to give themselves without reserve to Christ: "Most people think what the gospel needs is more clever, skilled people, when what it needs is more people who are willing to bleed, suffer, and die in a passion to see people come to Christ!"[6]

On September 6, 1978, Bob Pierce went home to heaven. Shortly before he died, he said, "I can tell you that, when you are just outside of heaven, all that matters is that you loved and served Jesus."[7]

After his death, tributes to Bob Pierce poured in from around the world. Torrey Johnson, founder of Youth for Christ, said, "I have never met a person with greater compassion." Billy Graham called him a champion of "the 'little people,' the forgotten, the hurting people who are unheard of and unsung except in the courts of heaven." Perhaps the most beautiful tribute was the simple phrase that appeared on the cover of *World Vision* magazine: "Bob Pierce, 1914–1978, Humanity's Friend."

CHAPTER 15

MAN WITH A MISSIONARY HEART

Pastor	Warren Shibley
Birth	1921 in Drumright, Oklahoma
Death	1965 in Tulsa, Oklahoma
Legacy	Warren Shibley was a Christian broadcaster, founding pastor of Gleaner Missionary Church, founder of Gleaner Bible College and Gleaner Missionary Society, composer, church planter, and world missions advocate. He published several articles, pamphlets, and *The Gleaner* magazine. With his wife, Lillian, they served as founding directors for the ministry of missionary-evangelist T. L. Osborn. Known as "the man with a missionary heart," Shibley led the church he founded in 1955 in giving half of every offering directly to missions. His son, David, founded the ministry of Global Advance.
Quote	Missions involvement isn't sentimental philanthropy. It's just an honest man paying his debt.

I will run the course of Your commandments, for You shall enlarge my heart (Ps. 119:32).

Warren Shibley was born in the little Oklahoma town of Drumright on March 4, 1921. His mother's parents had come to America from England, and his father had emigrated from Lebanon as a teenager.

Warren Shibley is a special hero of mine. You see, he's my father. His parents moved to the town of Bristow during the Oklahoma oil boom of the 1920s. Young Shibley, an excellent athlete, was named to the high school all-state teams in both football and basketball.

While he was in high school, Warren's mother experienced a deep spiritual renewal and began to urge him to go with her to church. Soon, Warren had opened his heart to Christ at the church's old-fashioned altar.

Warren was brought up in a patriotic atmosphere. His father, who had witnessed the horrors of civil war and famine before he came to America, was determined to give something back to his adopted country. So he ran for public office and became one of the first immigrants elected to the Oklahoma legislature.

> "Missions involvement isn't sentimental philanthropy. It's just an honest man paying his debt."
>
> ~ WARREN SHIBLEY ~

Warren's parents loved America so much that, when he was born, they named him after a president — Warren Harding Shibley.

Upon graduating from high school, Warren declined sports scholarship offers from several major colleges. Instead, he joined the U.S. Coast Guard and saw action in the South Pacific in World War II aboard the *USS Hutchinson*. Like most of his generation, he was reticent to talk about his experiences in the war. Only in the last few years have I learned that he was a gunner, helping protect his ship from kamikaze air raids by Japanese bombers. Also (not surprisingly) he was one of the leading scorers among the ship's basketball teams.

The war gave the small-town Oklahoma young man the opportunity to live on both coasts of the United States and see several Asian cultures. These experiences enlarged his compassion and missions vision.

While his shipmates would go out on leave, he would often stay alone on board ship, reading his Bible by a small light above his bunk and praying for a greater heart for the world.

Warren suffered a disability in his feet during the war, and friends urged him to take the disability money that was rightfully his. "My country doesn't owe me anything," he replied, "and I owe it a lot."

After the war, Warren returned home, realizing that his direction in life would never be the same. He could never again hide from the cries of a world that needed Jesus. Soon, he knew that his life must be devoted to getting the good news to others.

In January 1949 he married Lillian Roberts, the secretary of the church he attended. I was their first child, arriving in March the next year. Two sisters followed, in 1955 and 1957.

Warren Shibley was ordained as a minister of the gospel in 1953. In the next 12 years, he would pioneer a nationwide radio broadcast, start a church and Bible school in Tulsa, publish a monthly missions magazine, and establish the Gleaner Missionary Society. He and my mother also served as founding directors for the missionary evangelism ministry of T. L. Osborn.[1]

Our home was filled with missionary stories, visits from missionaries and national workers, and evening prayers for God's work worldwide. It was not unusual for me to awaken in the middle of the night to hear my father earnestly praying for nations and missionary friends.

He kept a relentless pace in his desire to see the gospel advanced, and he died at the young age of 44 in 1965. I have only good memories of a man completely committed to the Great Commission. Perhaps, in his zeal, he did not care for his body as he should have, but that verdict is heaven's to give. One thing is certain: Thousands will be in heaven because of his life and heart to minister worldwide.

He left me a rich missions heritage. Each time I board a plane to go somewhere to share Jesus, I remember that I'm reaping the harvest of a life sown to world missions.

He may have known his time was short. I don't know. But he would often recite this reminder to us:

Only one life;
'Twill soon be past.
Only what's done for Christ
will last.

CHAPTER 16

No Wild Beast Would Dare

Missionary	Mary Slessor
Birth	1848 in Aberdeen, Scotland
Death	1915 in rural Calabar (now Nigeria)
Legacy	Inspired by fellow Scottish missionary, David Livingstone, Mary Slessor became a pioneering missionary to Calabar in west Africa. Affectionately referred to by the indigenous people as the "Queen of Calabar," she courageously fought against poverty, superstition, and cruel practices associated with animistic religions. She rescued many twin babies who were traditionally consigned to death because they were perceived as cursed. She also helped their homeless mothers. Always she was a courageous evangelist of the gospel of Jesus Christ. For her landmark work in opening churches, schools, and medical outposts, she was named the first female vice consul in the British Empire.
Quote	Prayer is the greatest power God has put into our hands for service. Praying is harder than doing, at least I find it so, but the dynamic lies that way to advance the Kingdom.

I will speak of Your testimonies also before kings, and will not be ashamed (Ps. 119:46).

Late one night, a ship carrying Mary Slessor and three of her rescued children arrived from Britain in Calabar, West Africa. After disembarking, Mary immediately began walking through the dark, thick jungle with her children toward the missions compound she had established miles inland.

"Weren't you and the children afraid of being attacked by thieves or wild animals?" a friend inquired.

"No self-respecting lion would have dared attack us, the way we sang those hymns!" she replied.

Such was the courage of Mary Slessor, who was born in Dundee, Scotland, into an unhappy, poverty-stricken home. Her alcoholic father sometimes threw young Mary out of the house at night after he had been drinking. Still, she continued to go to school and work with her mother in the mills. By the time she was 14, Mary was the primary wage earner in the family. Her mother could no longer work outside the home, having given birth to her seventh child.

Mary received Christ at an early age and became interested in missions almost immediately. She was active in her Scottish Presbyterian church, teaching Sunday school and working in the church's Queen Street Mission, where she received valuable experience in sharing God's love with needy people.

When Mary was in her twenties, God used two events to lead her to become a missionary. First, Mary's brother John died, deeply grieving the family. Mary's mother had always hoped John would be a missionary. Mary now resolved to take John's place. News of the death of the great missionary-statesman David Livingstone sealed her decision. Here is the story:

> One day, there flashed through the land a telegram which caused much excitement and sorrow. Africa was then an unknown country, vast and mysterious, and haunted by all the horrors of slavery and heathenism. For a long time, there had been tramping through it a white man, a Scotsman, David Livingstone, hero of heroes, who had been gradually finding out the secrets of its lakes and rivers and peoples. Sometimes he was lost for years. The telegram which came told of his lonely death in a hut in the heart of the continent. Everyone asked: What is to be done now? Who is to take up the work of the great pioneer and help to save the natives from misery and death? Amongst those whose hearts leapt at the call was Mary Slessor.

She went to her mother. "Mother," she said, "I am going to offer myself as a missionary."

Mary Slessor was accepted by the Mission Board of the United Presbyterian Church in Edinburgh to go to Calabar as a teacher. "So she who had waited so long and so patiently, working within the walls of a factory, weaving the warp and woof in the loom, was now going to one of the wildest parts of Africa to weave there the lives of the people into new and beautiful patterns."[1]

At age 27, Mary Slessor sailed for Calabar — then part of the British Empire but now part of Nigeria in west Africa. Her first few years of missionary work were trying. Unhappy with her assignment of teaching in the mission school, Mary wanted to meet with people who had not yet heard of Jesus Christ. But tribal customs of witchcraft, superstition, and cruelty prevented the people from being interested in the message of the gospel.

> **"Prayer is the greatest power God has put into our hands for service. Praying is harder than doing, at least I find it so, but the dynamic lies that way to advance the Kingdom."**
>
> ~ MARY SLESSOR ~

Mary was particularly horrified by the tribal practice of murdering twin babies. The people believed that an evil spirit caused the birth of twins. So they killed the babies and cast out the mother from the tribe.

Mary began to rescue the twin babies and help their homeless mothers. Her involvement endangered her, but eventually led to reform among the tribes. In a letter to a Sunday school class in Dundee, Scotland, she described the moment when she learned the dreadful killings were over:

Just as it became dark one evening, I was sitting in my verandah talking to the children, when we heard the beating of drums and the singing of men coming near. This was strange, because we were on a piece of ground which no one in the town had a right to enter. Taking the wee twin boys in my hands, I rushed out, and what do you think I saw? A crowd of men standing outside the fence, chanting and swaying their bodies. They were proclaiming that all twins and twin-mothers could now live in the town, and that if anyone murdered the twins or harmed the mothers, he would be hanged by the neck. If you could have heard the twin-mothers who were there, how they laughed and clapped their hands and shouted, "Sosono! Sosono!" (Thank you! Thank you!) You will not wonder that amidst all the noise I turned aside and wept tears of joy and thankfulness, for it was a glorious day for Calabar.

A few days later the treaties were signed, and at the same time a new king was crowned. Twins' mothers were actually sitting with us on the platform in front of all the people.[2]

Mary finally determined to go into a rough, inland area called Okoyong, or the up-country of Calabar. Several missionaries had already been killed in the Okoyong region, and no single woman had ever dared to go there alone. But Mary Slessor was no ordinary person. She would lie awake at night planning ways to get behind the wall of bush. Hundreds of miles inland lay a vast region of forest and river into which white men had not ventured. She knew it would require courage and firmness on her part to combat the savage customs of the people. But Mary had no fear of harm because she wanted more than anything to tell them of Jesus' love for them.

Impressed with her courage, the king of the region helped Mary begin her pioneer missionary work, which continued for the next 25 years. Mary opened schools and medical outposts among the Okoyongs and acted as a judge, helping the people settle their quarrels. She became known as a peacemaker, an example of the words of Jesus: "Blessed are the peacemakers, for they shall be called sons of God" (Matt. 5:9).

Mary Slessor was named the first vice consul of Okoyong in 1892. She came to Calabar as a missionary, and her depth of commitment and willingness to challenge the boundaries of ordinary mission work earned her a position as the first woman vice consul in the British Empire.

Mary remained single throughout her life. She once accepted a marriage proposal from a missionary teacher, but because of his health, her fiancée would not have been able to live in the hardships of 19th-century Africa. Mary saw her work for Jesus as more important than marriage, and broke their engagement.

At age 55, Mary pioneered still another missions work in a new, unreached area. She spent the next ten years once again building churches, establishing schools, and telling people the story of Jesus. In 1915, at age 66, she died in a mud hut among the people she loved and served. Her testimony, however, lives on.

CHAPTER 17

PASSION FOR SOULS

Pastor	Oswald J. Smith
Birth	1889 in Ontario, Canada
Death	1986 in Toronto, Canada
Legacy	Many believe Oswald J. Smith was the greatest missions-hearted pastor in history. He founded The People's Church in Toronto which became the first church to give one million dollars in a single year to missions. He pioneered and championed the "faith promise" method of raising money for world missions. He was the author of 36 books and some 1200 poems, many of which were set to music. He was elected the first president of the Evangelical Fellowship of Canada.
Quote	Why should anyone hear the gospel twice until everyone has heard it once?

For God so loved the world that He gave His only begotten Son, that whoever believes in Him should not perish but have everlasting life (John 3:16).

When I was in high school, shortly after God had called me to preach, someone gave me a copy of *A Passion for Souls* by Oswald J. Smith. Each page seared its fire into my heart. I remember the first time I read Dr. Smith's piercing question, which still haunts me: "Why should anyone hear the gospel twice until everyone has heard it once?" After meeting Oswald J. Smith through his writings, my life was never the same.

One of the highest privileges of my life was meeting with Dr. Smith in person. I'll never forget that spring day in 1982 when I drove to his house in Toronto. Though elderly and bedfast, he had graciously consented to receive me. He greeted me warmly. Then, almost immediately, he asked, "Young man, what are you doing for missions?" I was glad to tell him of my ministry in many nations. Yet, in spite of my involvement, in the presence of this greatest living missionary statesman, I felt exceedingly humbled and that I was not doing enough.

Before I left, I asked him to pray. "Dr. Smith," I requested, "will you pray that your passion for souls will be transmitted to my generation?" His aged hand took mine, and he prayed heaven down to earth. That little bedroom became a cathedral for me that day.

Oswald J. Smith was born in a farmhouse on the plains of Ontario, Canada, on November 8, 1889, the eldest of ten children. He was raised in a God-fearing home where prayers and Bible reading were part of the daily routine. Young Oswald battled many sicknesses. Once, while he was fighting pneumonia, his teacher said this poor lad "would never live to see a mission field." Not only did Oswald J. Smith live, but he lived to be almost 100 years old! And not only did he see a mission field, he preached in 70 countries.

In 1906, while still in his teens, Oswald and his brother went to the great evangelistic campaigns in Toronto being conducted by R. A. Torrey. Dr. Torrey was the godly successor to D. L. Moody, and the second president of Moody Bible Institute. There, Oswald heard the gospel clearly presented. He gladly committed his life and future to Jesus Christ.

Soon he felt a clear call to gospel ministry. He enrolled in Toronto Bible College and did further study at Manitoba College. He also studied at McCormack Seminary in Chicago. Ordained as a Presbyterian minister, he became the associate pastor of Dale Presbyterian Church in Toronto in 1915.

Oswald was already ablaze with a passion to see people won to Christ. "I want Thy plan, O God, for my life," he prayed. "May I be happy and contented whether in the homeland or on the foreign field, whether married or alone, in happiness or sorrow, health or sickness, prosperity or adversity — I want Thy plan, O God, for my life. I want it; oh, I want it!"[1]

During his years at college and seminary, God was weaving a missions vision into Oswald. During his last term in seminary, he attended a missionary meeting where a map of the world was prominently displayed. From the map, he caught a fresh glimpse of the world's need for Christ. He realized that his ministry was to be worldwide. "I must be a missionary to the whole world," he wrote in his journal. "My own dear country calls me — would that I might set it on fire for God. But *the world is my parish*. Even if I live in one place, *I must reach beyond my local parish to the world*."

His vision to reach the unreached was also expanded during college when he sold Bibles to the Indians in the vast reaches of the Canadian north country. During this time, he began publishing gospel tracts and writing hymns.

On September 12, 1916, he married Daisy, a young deaconess, active in the ministry of Dale Presbyterian Church in Toronto. The next month he became acting pastor of the church. Oswald's strong commitment to world missions did not sit well with some members of the congregation. Oswald himself longed for a church where missions came first. He often said, "The supreme task of the church is the evangelization of the world."

In a time of prayer in 1919, God gave Oswald a vision for a church that would love all the different peoples of earth. Nine years later, the Peoples Church of Toronto, Canada, was established. Dr. Oswald J. Smith would lead the church through the next four decades as the pastor. Later, his son, Paul Smith, was the capable pastor of the church.

Oswald could not be confined to Toronto. Although he was a loyal church pastor, he viewed the church as his base of ministry, not the entire sphere of his ministry. From its beginning, he led the church in bold annual missions conferences. He was the first to use the "faith promise" method of raising money for missions on a large scale. Always, the challenge he placed before his congregation was that they could help reach the entire world from Toronto. He wrote, "I have seen

> "Why should anyone hear the gospel twice until everyone has heard it once?"
>
> ~ Oswald J. Smith ~

the vision and for self I cannot live; life is less than worthless till my all I give."

Oswald developed a simple, yet powerful, creed for his church:

> We believe in an unmutilated Bible; salvation through the blood of Christ; entire separation from the world; a Spirit-filled life for Christian service; victory over all known sin through the indwelling Christ; rugged consecration to sacrificial service; practical faith in the sufficiency of Christ for spiritual, temporal, and physical needs; the purifying hope of the Lord's return; and a burning missionary zeal for the bringing back of the King through world evangelization.[2]

The missions conferences of the Peoples Church drew hundreds, sometimes thousands, across North America. For many, it was *the* missions event of the year. In 1976, the church gave over a million dollars to missions, and it has continued to give heavily to missions enterprises.

By the early eighties, over $17 million had been raised and the church was helping support 242 missionaries and 222 national workers. Oswald J. Smith had a unique ability to convey his heart for the world to his people. This is not an easy assignment, as many pastors have discovered. But no one could deny his love for a lost world. "Oh, these teeming multitudes," he exclaimed. "How they have won me!"[3]

His son Paul often spoke of how his father was driven to reach the unreached. "All his strength and energy of body, soul, and mind," Paul said, "had to be channeled, contained. . . . Father had this sense of destiny."[4]

Oswald's 36 books have sold over six million copies and have been translated into 125 languages. He also wrote an amazing 1,200 hymns. "Then Jesus Came" and "The Song of the Soul Set Free" are among his most popular.

Oswald J. Smith received many honors over the years. He attained several honorary doctorates, the first from Asbury College in 1936. He was a member of the Royal Geographical Society, the Royal Society of Literature of the United Kingdom, and the

American Society of Composers, Authors, and Publishers. In 1965, the Evangelical Fellowship of Canada was formed with Oswald as first president.

Billy Graham said of him, "Oswald Smith has been a legend in his time. . . . My whole life and my ministry have been touched and directed by Oswald J. Smith."[5]

Nevertheless, even though he had become famous as a missionary statesman, he remained truly humble. Remembering God's goodness, he said, "The longer I live, the more unworthy I feel. The wonder of God's love becomes more overwhelming with the passing years."[6]

In his later years, he retained a rigorous schedule. More and more, he turned his focus to younger preachers. "You can produce only what you yourself are," he challenged them. "More than ever today, we need the unction of the Holy Spirit. . . . When the Holy Spirit takes control in a church, there will be blessing and unity and power. Souls will be saved. The gospel will go out."[7]

CHAPTER 18

WITHIN A YARD OF HELL

Missionary	C. T. Studd
Birth	1860 in Spratton, England
Death	1931 in Ibambi, Belgian Congo
Legacy	A renowned cricketer, C. T. Studd turned his back on fame and gave away much of his wealth to further Christian missions. He sailed to China as one of the famous Cambridge Seven, sparking great interest in world missions among college students. On a trip to the United States, he inspired many in the Student Volunteer Movement and became friends with John R. Mott. As an athlete, he was a proponent of "muscular Christianity," encouraging discipline and sacrifice for the cause of Christ. Along with Norman Grubb, he established the Worldwide Evangelization Crusade (now WEC International). He maintained a lifelong passion to see the Great Commission fulfilled. His primary focus was China, India, and Africa.
Quote	Some wish to live within the sound Of church and chapel bell; I want to run a rescue shop Within a yard of hell.

But what things were gain to me, these I have counted loss for Christ. Yet indeed I also count all things loss for the excellence of the knowledge of Christ Jesus my Lord, for whom I have suffered the loss of all things, and count them as rubbish, that I may gain Christ (Phil. 3:7–8).

C. T. Studd was born in the lap of luxury. His father, a wealthy retired planter in India, had returned to England and the leisure of Tedworth, the family estate in Wiltshire. Young C. T. was given the best of British education at Eton and Cambridge.

During college, he was captain of the famous Cambridge cricket team, an English sport similar to baseball. Some people thought C. T. was England's greatest cricketer.

In 1877, his father committed his life to Christ at an evangelistic meeting conducted by the famed American evangelist D.L. Moody. The following year, all three of Mr. Studd's sons were converted. C. T. took an interest in foreign missions and, about six months after his conversion, dedicated his life to missionary service at another meeting conducted by Moody.

While a student at Trinity College at Cambridge, his popularity as a cricketer helped him influence other students. Six other Cambridge students answered the call to missions with C. T. Together they became known as the Cambridge Seven and decided to sail to China to work with Hudson Taylor. One newspaper commented, "Never before in the history of missions has so unique a band set out to labor in the foreign field."[1]

Not everyone supported C. T.'s decision to become a missionary. Cambridge students thought C. T. should pursue a career as a professional cricket player. Even members of his family questioned his move to foreign soil. Yet C. T. persisted and sailed for China with the China Inland Mission in 1885. There he met Priscilla Steward, a missionary with the Salvation Army. They were married after a brief courtship and would someday have four daughters, all born in China.

The Studds' mission was difficult. At that time, few people were trying to help those tormented by drug abuse. C. T. could not stand by; he had to help. The Chinese were not receptive, however, and when C. T. and Priscilla stepped outside their house, they were often besieged with angry cursing from the people. But C. T. continued his work with the drug addicts while Priscilla continued her work with women.

Ill health forced C. T. to return to England. While he recuperated, he traveled and preached to masses of students, who flocked to hear him both in Britain and America. Hundreds committed themselves to missionary service. And his efforts influenced the beginning of the Student Volunteer Movement in America.

After six years, he returned overseas, this time to India, where he pastored for several years. Again, he was forced to return home because of illness.

It seemed impossible, however, for C. T. Studd not to be engaged in missionary work. Priscilla

was suffering from a heart condition, and C. T. himself was far from healthy. Nevertheless, he struck out again for missionary soil — this time his destination was Africa. This once-wealthy man was now 50 years old, in poor health, and had little financial support. Although he was heir to a large inheritance, he gave it all away to missionary work so he could live as a "faith missionary."

C. T.'s work in central Africa was a mixture of successes and failures. His actions were sometimes questioned, even by his most loyal supporters. He appeared to be overly strict on himself and others. He required the missionaries to live an African lifestyle, avoiding any appearance of European affluence. He called this the cost of full commitment to the Lord and His work. Although his commitment to Christ was a positive influence, his stubborn determination sometimes had negative results. Never relaxing in zeal or in effort, he labored long hours with no breaks, and he had little sympathy for those who did not do the same. This cost C. T. his health as well as the support of fellow missionaries and national workers whom he injured with his insensitive remarks.

No one ever questioned C. T. Studd's unshakable commitment to the task of evangelizing the world. Along with co-worker Norman Grubb, C. T. established the Worldwide Evangelization Crusade (WEC). Today, WEC continues to reach around the globe with hundreds of missionaries.

C. T. Studd saw no sacrifice as too great for the advance of the gospel. He gave up fortune and fame in athletics. He surrendered time with his wife and family. He worked tirelessly, and for all this he was sometimes misunderstood. Yet he never retreated from his missionary call: "If Jesus Christ be God and died for me, then no sacrifice is too great for me to give for Him."[2]

CHAPTER 19

THE EXCHANGED LIFE

Missionary	Hudson Taylor
Birth	1832 in Barnsley, England
Death	1905 in Changsha, Hunan, China
Legacy	J. Hudson Taylor was a legendary missionary to China and founder of China Inland Mission (now OMF International). By 1891 Taylor had helped recruit some 640 workers. He was ahead of his time in cross-cultural sensitivity, adopting local dress and many Chinese customs. He helped launch the era of "faith missions." Taylor was known for his reliance on God and "the exchanged life." Some mission historians believe he was the most fruitful missionary since the apostle Paul. Biographies which chronicled Taylor's fervor and pioneering audacity inspired many notable missionaries including Amy Carmichael, Eric Liddell, Jim Elliot, and evangelist Billy Graham.
Quote	We are a supernatural people born again by a supernatural birth, kept by a supernatural power; sustained on supernatural food, taught by a supernatural Teacher from a supernatural Book. We are led by a supernatural Captain in right paths to assured victories.

I have been crucified with Christ; it is no longer I who live, but Christ lives in me; and the life which I now live in the flesh I live by faith in the Son of God, who loved me and gave Himself for me (Gal. 2:20).

"No other missionary in the 19 centuries since the Apostle Paul has had a wider vision and has carried out a more systematized plan of evangelizing a broad geographical area than Hudson Taylor,"[1] wrote missionary biographer Ruth Tucker. With the possible exception of David Livingstone, no one life has challenged more people for missionary service.

Hudson Taylor was born in Yorkshire, England, in 1832. His father was a Methodist lay preacher and pharmacist. When he was only five years old, young Hudson believed God wanted him to be a missionary. When amused relatives and friends would ask where, his immediate reply was "China."

God gave Hudson this vivid insight into his future. Yet Hudson did not come into a personal relationship with Jesus Christ until he was 17. After reading a gospel tract, he was intensely convicted of his need for the Savior, and immediately committed his life to Christ. Hudson's mother, away on a two-week trip, was not at all surprised when she returned and heard of his conversion. At the exact hour of his commitment, though miles away, she had been praying for him, deeply burdened. When the burden lifted, she knew Hudson had given his heart to Christ.

Here is how Hudson later described their meeting. "When our dear mother came home a fortnight later, I was the first to meet her at the door, and to tell her I had such glad news to give. She said, 'I know, my boy; I have been rejoicing for a fortnight in the glad tiding you have to tell me.' "[2]

Soon the whisperings in his heart for China returned, more intensely than ever. He began to study medicine, hoping that a medical degree might open China's door to him. He also imposed on himself a sparse diet and rugged lifestyle, believing this would prepare him for the years ahead.

"Having now the twofold object in view of accustoming myself to endure hardness and economizing in order to be able more largely to assist others," he later recalled, "I soon found that I could live upon very much less than I had previously thought possible."[3]

Finally, the day came when he set sail for China, arriving in Shanghai in 1854. But his lofty vision to quickly evangelize China's millions was soon weighted with the discouragements of learning the difficult language, receiving limited support, and enduring disapproval from the older missionaries. Hudson did not give up, however; he had committed himself to God and to this work.

Traveling into the interior of China where no other missionary had gone, he was disappointed to find that the people were more interested in his different dress than in his message. There seemed to be only one solution: he would dress Chinese! Hudson shaved part of his head and braided and dyed his remaining hair. His plan worked! The Chinese began to respond when he told them of Christ.

During this time, he met Maria Dyer. Born of missionary parents in China, she had received her schooling in England, and returned to China in her late teens. Maria's protective teacher, Mrs. Aldersey, did not approve of Hudson's "improper" manners — going against established missionary customs and dressing like the Chinese — and almost ruined their romance. Eventually, the young couple was able to marry on January 20, 1858.

> "We are a supernatural people born again by a supernatural birth, kept by a supernatural power; sustained on supernatural food, taught by a supernatural Teacher from a supernatural Book. We are led by a supernatural Captain in right paths to assured victories."
>
> ~ HUDSON TAYLOR ~

Hudson and his new wife were happy in their joint ministry, but Hudson realized he needed more medical training. This need, along with his weakening health, sent the Taylors back to England for an extended furlough. It proved to be no vacation, however. Hudson often worked up to 15 hours a day, revising the New Testament in the Ningpo language. Habits of discipline and organization, learned years earlier, were now paying off and would be even more valuable in the days ahead.

While in England, Hudson's heart burned more passionately than ever to see the gospel reach every person in China. Therefore, he challenged Christians across England to pray, give, and go to China where "a million souls each month" were going into eternity without Christ. During this time, the vision for the China Inland Mission (CIM) was born in Hudson's heart. In 1865, CIM officially began its ministry. The next year, Hudson left with the largest group of missions recruits ever to set sail up to that time. He reasoned that "twenty-four willing, skillful laborers" would provide the needed manpower to put two missionaries in each unreached province in China.

Disunity almost dashed noble venture. New recruits were offended at having to wear Chinese dress, and questioned Hudson's decision as leader of the new mission. The untimely death of the Taylors' daughter Gracie brought some temporary healing to the strained relations. The discontent was eventually traced to one couple and two sisters. When they left, a cooperative spirit was restored and the China Inland Mission expanded rapidly.

Tragedies multiplied for the Taylors. A young son died. The family went through the pain of the surviving children's departure for England and school. Another baby was born but lived less than two weeks. A few days after his death, Maria died at the age of 33.

On top of these personal sorrows, deep feelings of resentment mounted against the missionaries. Age-old Chinese hostility against foreigners was magnified in the interior. Riots broke out in Yangchow in 1868. The missionaries' home was burned to the ground.

In the midst of this intense pain, Hudson Taylor sought a deeper walk with God. He found the encouragement he needed in the letter of a friend dated Saturday, September 4, 1869. Hudson's friend urged him to exchange all his weaknesses for the strength of Christ.

He summarized this exchanged life by writing, "To *let* my loving Savior work in me *His will*. . . . Abiding, not striving or struggling. . . . Not a striving to have faith or to increase our faith, but a looking at the faithful One seems all we need."[4] Hudson determined he would learn to abide in Christ and claim his position in Him. He announced, "God has made me a new man."

The following year, Hudson married Jennie Faulding, a 27-year-old missionary. Jenny served the China Inland Mission faithfully, and even led a group of missionary women into an unreached part of the interior.

Hudson Taylor's influence for world evangelization continued to grow. In his own lifetime, he would see CIM dispatch almost 700 missionaries to China. His writings were widely read and his travels brought him wide acclaim. In many ways, he was ahead of his time. He radically identified with the people. He believed the best place to direct the work of missions was in the field, not from a headquarters thousands of miles away. And he helped launch the era of "faith missions," where missionaries trust God for their support. "God's work done in God's way will not lack God's supply," he said.[5]

Henry Frost, a co-worker with Hudson, paid tribute to him on the centennial anniversary of his birth. He cited several characteristics that placed Hudson Taylor and his work at the top of missionary effectiveness. Among those characteristics Frost noted:

- His intellect. "He read the Old Testament in the original Hebrew and the New in the original Greek. . . . he had a masterly grip of the principles of medicine and surgery, to the blessing and actual saving of many lives in China. . . . He was proficient in the Chinese language, in two dialects. He had in marked measure the capacity of analysis and synthesis."

- His naturalness. "Great men do not have to strive to be great; they simply are great. And because Mr. Taylor was great, he was simple. . . . When he prayed he did not preach; he spoke as a child to his father."

- His faith. "Mr. Taylor never spoke of his faith, he talked about God's faithfulness. Taylor's definition of faith: 'Faith is reckoning on God's faithfulness.'"

- His holiness. "I never saw Mr. Taylor through all the years I knew him when I had any reason to suppose that he was out of fellowship with God. This is a great thing to be able to say of a mortal man."[6]

In 1900, the most terrible slaughter in the history of missions began in China. A decree from Beijing ordered the death of all foreigners. Any hint of Christianity was to be uprooted from the country. One hundred and thirty-five missionaries and 53 missionary children were killed. Those who suffered worst were often CIM missionaries.

By then, Hudson was elderly and trying to regain his health in Switzerland. The shocking news was almost too much for him. He never fully recovered from the grief. He died one month after returning to his beloved China.

The work that Hudson began, however, continued to grow. In 1964, the China Inland Mission celebrated 100 years of missionary service, and changed its name to the Overseas Missionary Fellowship. Today it is known as OMF International. This ministry remains today an eloquent testimony to the faith and love for souls that were Hudson Taylor's. Here, indeed, was a rare man. Henry Frost also wrote a poem to celebrate Taylor's life. The final lines read:

> The dreamer died; they laid him 'neath the sod —
> But now a countless host adores his God![7]

CHAPTER 20

Does God Speak My Language?

Missionary	William Cameron Townsend
Birth	1896 in Eastvale, California
Death	1982 in Waxhaw, North Carolina
Legacy	Cameron Townsend was the visionary founder of Wycliffe Bible Translators, the Summer Institute of Linguistics (SIL), and the Jungle Aviation and Radio Service (JAARS). He promoted Bible translation and literacy among minority language groups. Townsend helped change the paradigm of missions. Mission historians see the inaugural meeting of Camp Wycliffe (which later became SIL) in a small Arkansas town in 1934 as a landmark in Christian missions. His vision for Bible translation in every language has spawned many other ministries including Evangel Bible Translators and The Seed Company.
Quote	The greatest missionary is the Bible in the mother tongue. It never needs a furlough, is never considered a foreigner.

You were slain, and have redeemed us to God by Your blood out of every tribe and tongue and people and nation (Rev. 5:9).

William Cameron Townsend, lovingly known by millions as "Uncle Cam," was ahead of his time with his different approach to mission works. His fresh ideas were not always accepted, however. Through the years, he received both lavish praise and harsh criticism. Despite disapproval, Uncle Cam was accepting and tolerant of Christians with opposing views and of non-Christians. Cam believed that cooperation among Christians was a must if the Bible was to be translated into new languages. The message of the Bible would change cultures, he maintained, so getting God's Word to the people was his first concern. Cam's commitment to taking God's Word to those who had never heard it led to the founding of three vital ministries: the Wycliffe Bible Translators, the Summer Institute of Linguistics, and the Jungle Aviation and Radio Service.

Although his family did not have much money, they had a rich faith in God. At the Townsend farm in California, one book stood above all others — the Bible. Each morning Cam's father would read chapters out of the Bible to his children. Family devotions included Bible reading, a hymn, and a prayer. Cam's father always ended his prayer with, "May the knowledge of the Lord cover the earth as the waters cover the sea."

Godly character and love for those who needed the gospel were planted early inside young Townsend. It is little wonder that during his second year of college, he accepted an assignment to sell Bibles in Guatemala. Cam's missions enthusiasm was heightened when John R. Mott, a leader of the Student Volunteer Movement, spoke at his campus. He was further inspired by the life of Hudson Taylor. Taylor's pioneering spirit appealed to Townsend. If God called him to be a missionary, Cam thought, he wanted to be like Hudson Taylor.

Cam's trip to Guatemala was the beginning of a missionary career that would last more than 50 years. What he found in Guatemala troubled him. He saw that the Spanish Bibles he was trying to sell were not understood by the Indians of the rural areas. They could neither read nor speak Spanish. Cam settled among the 200,000 Cakchiquel Indians. Their confusing language had never been reduced to writing, so Cam embarked on the task. For the next 13 years, he lived among the people, learning and writing their language. In 1929, after ten years of hard work, Cam completed the New Testament in the Cakchiquel language.

He knew he had found his life's calling. He felt that the people throughout the world who had no Bibles were asking, "Does God speak my language?" He would search them out and work to get God's Word to them. Cam soon realized that Bible translation had often been an important part of missions work. William Carey, Adoniram Judson, and Hudson Taylor were all Bible translators. But seldom had Bible translation been seen as the first job to be done.

While in Guatemala, Cam met and married Elvira Malmstrom, a first-term missionary also serving there. A valuable aide in Bible translation, she served the Lord faithfully and worked her way through the challenges of missionary life. Unfortunately, she died at a young age in 1944.

Cam's life with the Cakchiquel convinced him that missions work should focus on the unreached peoples of the world. He was deeply moved by Jesus' words of Luke 15:4: "What man of you, having a hundred sheep, if he loses one of them, does not leave the ninety-nine in the wilderness, and go after the one which is lost until he finds it?"

"Well, Lord," Cam prayed, "that settles it. Unless You definitely lead me down a different path . . . then I'm going to the one percent."

Cam finally decided to do something about his burden to train others to take the Bible to those without it. With the help of a friend, L. L. Letgers, he formed Camp Wycliffe on a farm in the Ozark Mountain village of Sulphur Springs, Arkansas. There, the small band of recruits learned the basic skills of linguistics, and the science of languages and how they are written. The farm property was owned by John Brown University, a few miles away. This was the beginning of a strong friendship between that Christian school and Wycliffe Bible Translators (WBT), which continues to the present. The few people in the little farmhouse probably could not conceive that they were on the ground floor of what would grow to be one of the largest independent Protestant missions organizations.

Only a year later, Cam's first Bible translators were sent to work among tribes in Mexico. In 1942, the Wycliffe Bible Translators, which received its name from John Wycliffe, the 14th-century English Bible translator, and its sister organization,

> "The greatest missionary is the Bible in the mother tongue. It never needs a furlough, is never considered a foreigner."
>
> ~ WILLIAM CAMERON TOWNSEND ~

the Summer Institute of Linguistics (SIL), were formed. Another helping ministry, Jungle Aviation and Radio Service (JAARS) was launched to help get the translators to their remote assignments.

Uncle Cam despised any bigotry or race prejudice and he urged non-white people to apply as Wycliffe translators. In a time when most missions agencies would not even consider it, Uncle Cam sent out two single women as a missionary team. In 1950, Wycliffe sent Loretta Anderson and Doris Cox to the headhunting Shapra tribe in Peru. The chief of the tribe, Tairi, had gained his position by murdering the former chief. But the Christian women won the hearts of the Shapras and the respect of the chief. Tairi even began helping them learn the language, and later turned away from murder and witchcraft and became a Christian. Many in the tribe followed their chief's example.

"If you had sent men," Tairi later told Uncle Cam, "we would have killed them on sight. Or if a couple, I'd have killed the man and taken the woman for myself. But what could a great chief do with two harmless girls who insisted on calling him brother?"[1]

In 1946, he married Elaine Mielke, whose work as a teacher in Chicago's schools had won her acclaim as Chicago's Outstanding Young Protestant. They were married in the home of General Cordons, former president of Mexico, and a close friend of Uncle Cam's. Uncle Cam and Elaine served 17 years in Peru where their four children were born. Then they pioneered a new work in Colombia.

After 50 years as a missionary, it would seem logical for Uncle Cam to consider retirement. However, that was not his nature. Here is what happened, as related in his biography:

> As Cam looked back on the fifty years since he'd gone to Guatemala, the old litchi tree seemed somehow symbolic of the tremendous growth of the work God had for him all along. His eyes were again on the future. "Elaine and I want to invest our next years where they will count the most."[2]

Thus, Uncle Cam found himself in the Soviet Union, studying Russian and opening discussions for Bible translation for the many languages spoken by people in the Caucasus.

Cameron Townsend not only left behind one of the largest missions organizations in the world, but he influenced many who would start similar movements. Syvelle Phillips is president of Evangel Bible Translators, a group which seeks to recruit nationals around the world in Bible translation. "I was a successful pastor in California when I met Uncle Cam," Phillips says, "but because of his encouragement, I've given my life to getting God's Word to the Bible-less peoples of the world."[3]

Through the years, Uncle Cam received many honors, often from governments in nations where SIL was helping reduce illiteracy. Offered honorary doctorates by several American universities, he declined them, fearing it would separate him from the people he wanted to serve.

Today, those involved with Wycliffe and SIL number about 5,300. Their combined efforts have produced some 578 completed translations of the New Testament. About 20 to 25 new translations are completed yearly. However, the job is far from finished — the Bible has been translated into less than half of the 6,800 languages in the world.

At the time of Cam's death in 1982, tributes poured in from all over the world. Ralph Winter, founder of the U.S. Center for World Mission, placed him with William Carey and Hudson Taylor as one of the three most outstanding missionaries of the last 200 years. Billy Graham called him "the greatest missionary of our time." But Uncle Cam himself had another opinion: "The greatest missionary is the Bible in the mother tongue. It never needs a furlough, is never considered a foreigner."[4]

CHAPTER 21

THE NAVIGATOR

Mission Leader	Dawson Trotman
Birth	1906 in Bisbee, Arizona
Death	1956 in Schroon Lake, New York
Legacy	Dawson Trotman founded The Navigators in 1933, first working with sailors. Trotman was equally zealous for evangelism and the maturing of believers. His Scripturally based principles of discipleship continue to be used worldwide. Based on 2 Timothy 2:2, he taught and practiced "each one teach one." Not only did he grow the ministry of The Navigators, he gave himself tirelessly to helping other ministries. His early encouragement of Billy Graham, Bill Bright, and others became pivotal in the success of their ministries.
Quote	We've got the truth to dispel this darkness. We've got to get it out, out, OUT.

And the things that you have heard from me among many witnesses, commit these to faithful men who will be able to teach others also (2 Tim. 2:2).

Dawson Trotman was one of the most creative persons of the 20th century, a pacesetter. Not only did he pioneer a certain style of ministry, but he invented new words to describe it. The term "follow-up" was probably unknown before Dawson. He made the word "Timothy" not only a proper noun but a verb to describe an older Christian training a younger one. For a sailor's spiritual food, he must take his "B rations" (Bible rations).

Trotman would be used of God to cross paths with men of

vision, such as Jim Rayburn (who founded Young Life), Cameron Townsend (who started Wycliffe Bible Translators), Bill Bright (the founder of Campus Crusade for Christ), and Billy Graham. Each had separate visions, yet all were united in a drive for "world evangelization in this generation."

Dawson passionately supported the Great Commission. He believed that obedience to the mandate from Matthew 28:19–20 involved more than preaching the gospel to every creature. He was committed to making disciples, followers of Christ, from all nations.

Dawson Earl Trotman was born on March 25, 1906, in Bisbee, Arizona. A charmer, he had become the master of the double standard by the time he was in high school. As valedictorian of his graduating class, he spoke on "Morality vs. Legality," while stealing from school funds.

Dawson had little time for the half-hearted religion of his father and what he perceived to be his mother's fanatic religion. He continued to have brushes with the law. Much of this trouble stemmed from a growing abuse of alcohol. Yet his mother fervently prayed for him and urged others to join her.

A Christian neighbor called Mrs. Trotman to encourage her not to worry about Dawson: "The Lord showed me a vision of Dawson holding a Bible, speaking to a large group of people, and the burden has lifted," she said. "Don't worry about Dawson anymore."[1]

These prayers were soon answered. As a member of a Presbyterian youth group, Dawson had to memorize Scripture to gain points for his team in competition. The living Word worked in Dawson's heart. One day he memorized John 5:24: "He who hears My word and believes in Him who sent Me has everlasting life." Dawson prayed, "Oh, God, that's wonderful — everlasting life. Oh, God, whatever this means, I want to have it. Whatever it means to receive Jesus, I'll do it right now!"[2]

Immediately, Dawson was completely committed to Jesus Christ and His cause. He formed clubs for young boys to memorize Bible verses and high school clubs that also stressed the importance of the Bible. "Immediately after my conversion," Dawson recalled, "I began learning verses, and I learned one a day for the first three years. In those years, I learned my first thousand verses."

Soon after his conversion, he met and began to date Lila Clayton, and they were married July 3, 1932. Dawson wanted further training and enrolled in the Bible Institute of Los Angeles and the Los Angeles Baptist Theological Seminary. He was a good student and especially enjoyed Charles Fuller's class on Romans.

Determined to be God's man, he challenged a friend to spend a month with him in prayer in the mountains overlooking Los Angeles at five o'clock each morning. Taking a map with them, they prayed that God would use them to minister in neighboring cities.

As their faith increased, they began to pray for a ministry across America, mentioning the states by name. Soon they found themselves praying for the privilege of preaching the gospel to the nations of the world, again mentioning nations by name. Little did they realize they were laying the spiritual groundwork for a worldwide movement. Within a decade they would see fulfillment of these prayers.

The Trotmans began to open their home to sailors who were stationed in the Los Angeles area. Out of this ministry came the first Navigators Bible study groups. Dawson trained these young sailors to share their faith in Christ.

Many Navigator men would later sail to the Pacific, and some lost their lives in battle during World War II. After the war, when the *California* was raised from the depths of Pearl Harbor, the body of a Navigator, Francis Cole, was found on his bunk with an open Bible. He was probably talking with his bunkmate about Christ at the time of the Japanese attack on December 7, 1941.

Dawson was constantly on the lookout for ways to make the Bible's truth real to those with whom he shared. In 1930, he designed a wheel representing the obedient Christian life, with balanced spokes of the Word, prayer, witness, and fellowship. Seventy years later, it is still probably the most widely used follow-up illustration.

Dawson loved the Bible, calling it "God's great love letter to humanity." And he taught the "H.W.L.W." principle — "His Word the last word." Dawson contended that our last thoughts before we go to sleep at night should be from God's Word.

The great principle of his life was what he called the "2:2 principle" from 2 Timothy. Dawson was constantly training others in the Christian life. He believed this was a great key to finishing the missionary task. He called it "reproducing reproducers." In other words, a person should share his faith with others and train them to do the same.

With every year, Dawson's fire for world evangelization grew. On an overseas trip, he saw many people engaged in religious practices with no reality of Christ in their lives. He wrote back to his young Navigators, "Kids, we've got the truth to dispel this darkness. We've got to get it out, out, OUT!"[3]

He constantly looked for better methods of sharing the gospel with others. He knew that the problem was not with the message itself. "The reason that we are not getting this gospel to the ends of the earth is not because it's not potent enough," he declared.

Dawson believed the great need was for committed young lives. "What is the need of the hour?" he asked. "It is to believe that our God controls the universe and that when He said, 'the earth shall be filled with the glory of the Lord as the waters cover the sea,' He meant it."[4]

Throughout his life, Dawson would give himself not only to the growth of the Navigators ministry, but to anyone who was involved in world missions. His life touched the ministries of Overseas Crusades, Word of Life, Campus Crusade for Christ, J. Edwin Orr's Brazil crusades, scores of Billy Graham crusades, Wycliffe Bible Translators, Young Life, Missionary Aviation Fellowship, Christian Businessmen's Committee, and Youth for Christ. He also was in close contact with Charles E. Fuller of the "Old-Fashioned Revival Hour." His close friend Erwin Moon produced the Sermons from Science films sponsored by the Moody Bible Institute.

At the East Coast Navigators Conference in 1956, Dawson drowned in a boating accident. The boat, carrying a group of skiers, suddenly wheeled in a fast right turn and then smashed against a wave. The impact threw Dawson and a young woman, Aileen Beck, overboard. Dawson held Aileen above the water until the others could rescue her. By the time the crew reached out to help Dawson, he had lost all his strength and they were too late.

When Billy Graham was informed of Dawson's death, he blurted, "Oh, God, help me to rededicate my life!"

Ever committed to doing the job well for the Lord, Dawson encouraged thousands in their walk with Christ. Perhaps *Time* magazine's tribute best describes him: "Always Holding Someone Up."[5]

CHAPTER 22

TO WIN FOR THE LAMB

Mission Leader	Nikolaus Ludwig von Zinzendorf
Birth	1700 in Dresden, Germany
Death	1760 in Herrnhut, Germany
Legacy	Nikolaus Zinzendorf was a German Lutheran nobleman who gave spiritual leadership to the Moravian missionary movement. He provided refugees from Moravia to settle on his large estate in 1722 and infused them with missionary zeal. First as a benefactor he then became the spiritual visionary. A move of God's Spirit at Herrnhut in 1727 sparked a fire for world missions and spawned a prayer meeting that continued non-stop for more than 100 years. He leveraged his wealth and influence for the advance of the gospel, inspiring William Wilberforce and others to do the same.
Quote	May the Lamb that was slain receive the reward of His suffering!

And looking at Jesus as He walked, he said, "Behold the Lamb of God!" (*John 1:36*).

Nikolaus Ludwig von Zinzendorf was born into a wealthy family of the Austrian nobility. His father, a high government official, died early in Nikolaus's youth. When his mother remarried, he was sent to be raised by relatives who were deeply spiritual. At the age of ten, Nikolaus sat under the preaching of the Lutheran pastor August Hermann Francke, in Halle. There, together with other young boys, Nikolaus committed himself to "love the whole human family" and to spread the gospel.

With five other boys, he formed the Order of the Grain of Mustard Seed. The six friends were bound together in prayer. Their purpose was to witness for Christ, draw Christians together in fellowship, help those who were persecuted for their faith, and spread the message of Jesus in other lands.

While still a young man, Nikolaus was one day touring an art gallery when he was captivated by a Domenico Feti painting called *Behold the Man*. It depicted Christ's suffering with the crown of thorns, and the inscription on the painting read, "All this I did for you. What are you doing for Me?"

Nikolaus was immediately struck by the question. He knew he could no longer be happy living the life of a carefree nobleman. From then on, he would seek to live only for the Savior who had died for him. Soon he purchased an estate where, in 1722, he invited a group of refugees to form a Christian community which they called *Herrnhut*, meaning "the Lord's Watch."

In 1727, the Christian community at Herrnhut experienced a powerful awakening. The highlight was a communion service which, according to accounts of the event, signaled the coming of the Holy Spirit to the community. This ignited a fire for world missions. From this renewal a prayer meeting began which continued around the clock without interruption for more than 100 years!

Throughout his life, Nikolaus would point people past world missions to the reason for reaching out to others. He often said, "I have one passion only. It is He! It is He!" Urged by Nikolaus to "win for the Lamb those whom His blood has purchased," his Moravian followers became the most missions-minded Christian group of the 18th century. A high percentage of their membership was always serving Christ overseas. It was not uncommon for Moravians even to sell themselves into slavery, as they said, for the privilege of sharing Christ with the slaves for whom

Christ died.

Nikolaus himself served as a missionary and pastor. However, his most lasting influence is as a missionary statesman. For 33 years, he was the overseer of a worldwide group of missionaries who looked to him for counsel and inspiration.

In many ways, Nikolaus was a forerunner of the great missionary movement that would follow in the next century. We remember him as a man who was the driving force behind a church consumed by their love for Jesus and therefore, world missions. He was constantly urging the Moravians to reach into areas yet unreached with the gospel. He used his wealth and influence to motivate people in many areas of the world to open new regions to the Christian message. He said, "That land is henceforth my country which most needs the gospel."[1]

CHAPTER 23

APOSTLE TO ISLAM

Missionary	Samuel Zwemer
Birth	1867 in Vriesland, Michigan
Death	1952 in New York City, New York
Legacy	Known as "the apostle to Islam," Samuel Zwemer's tireless advocacy for getting the gospel to the Islamic world stirred Western Christians to see both the need and strategic challenge of evangelization among Muslims. His many books include a biography of Raymond Lull, the first Protestant missionary among Muslims. In addition to his personal missionary work in Arab nations, he was a motivator for world missions and a respected scholar. He taught missions and history of world religions at Princeton Seminary and other institutions. Missiologist J. Christy Wilson stated, "Robert Speer and Samuel Zwemer probably influenced more young men and women to go into missionary service than any two individuals in all of Christian history."
Quote	It was the bigness of the task and its difficulty that thrilled the early Church. Its apparent impossibility was its glory, its worldwide character, its grandeur. The same is true today.

And other sheep I have which are not of this fold; them also I must bring, and they will hear My voice; and there will be one flock and one shepherd (John 10:16).

"Do not pray for easy lives," Phillips Brooks once said. "Pray to be stronger men. Do not pray for tasks equal to your powers; pray for powers equal to your tasks."[1]

Samuel Zwemer did not have an easy life. But God granted him powers equal to his tasks.

Born near Holland, Michigan, of Dutch immigrant parents in 1867, Samuel was the 13th of 15 children. His father was a pastor in the Reformed Church. Four brothers followed their father as pastors, and a sister served 40 years as a missionary in China.

While a student at Hope College, Zwemer heard missionary-statesman Robert Wilder challenge students to reach unevangelized parts of the world with the gospel. God stirred Zwemer's heart for one of the most difficult of all mission fields, the Muslim world.

A Muslim is a believer in Islam, a religion based on the teachings of the prophet Mohammed, or Muhammad, who wrote the sacred book of their religion, the Koran. Millions of people today practice the religion of Islam, especially in North Africa, the Middle East, and southeast Asia.

Islam is an Arabic word meaning "surrender to God's will." Zwemer knew that millions of sincere Muslims wanted to know God's true will for them and that they needed to hear the good news of God's love and forgiveness through Jesus Christ. He also knew that Muslims are strong in their faith and it would be a big challenge to convert them — to do so would be "the glory of the impossible." Zwemer humbly believed that the task might be impossible for human strength but possible by the Holy Spirit.

Though denied by his church's missions board, Zwemer and another student volunteer, James Cantine, formed their own American Arabian Mission. After traveling across much of America to raise funds for the mission, Samuel Zwemer sailed for Arabia in 1890. Members of his group became some of the first Christian missionaries to Muslims in modern times. Few Christians had reached out to the Muslim world in love since the ministry of Raymond Lull in the 13th century. Most Muslims remembered only the cruelty of people calling themselves Christians who invaded the Muslims' lands in the Crusades of the Middle Ages.

Zwemer's work among the followers of Mohammed was slow and hard. But in 1895, he married a missionary nurse from England, Amy Wikes. The Zwemers continued their work among the people of the Persian Gulf, especially in the islands of Bahrain.

Although they tirelessly shared the message of Jesus, there was little response. Their discouragement was coupled with grief as two daughters, ages four and seven, died within eight days of each other in 1904.

Still, they did not give up. "We must follow in His footprints," Zwemer wrote. "The pioneer missionary, in overcoming obstacles and difficulties, has the privilege not only of knowing Christ and the power of His resurrection, but also something of the fellowship of His suffering."[2]

> "It was the bigness of the task and its difficulty that thrilled the early Church. Its apparent impossibility was its glory, its worldwide character, its grandeur. The same is true today."
>
> ~ SAMUEL ZWEMER ~

By 1905, Zwemer's ministry to the Arab world had established four mission stations. Only a few had been won to Christ, but they were very bold and shared their faith.

In 1906, Zwemer was asked to be the chairman of the first general missionary conference on Islam that convened in Cairo, Egypt. He also helped call a second conference, held in Lucknow, India, in 1911, for those who served in Muslim lands. Zwemer was now recognized as the leading authority on ministry to Muslims. In 1912, after much prayer, he accepted a call from several missions agencies to move to Cairo and coordinate the missions activity in the entire Muslim world. He continued to speak and write in behalf of the mission to Muslims. For 40 years he edited the *Moslem World* (an English journal), and he wrote nearly 50 books and hundreds of tracts. His sleep was often interrupted by the necessity to write.

Much of his writing was directed to Muslims themselves, explaining the message of salvation through Jesus Christ. Once, an angered Muslim teacher ripped to small pieces one of Zwemer's printed booklets in front of his class. One student became curious as to what kind of powerful message would cause such anger and fear. Later, he picked up pieces of the torn booklet and put it back together. After reading the booklet, he became a Christian.

Zwemer made Cairo his headquarters for 17 years. From there he traveled the world in behalf of missions to Muslims, raising money and starting work among Muslims in India, China, Indochina, and South Africa. Although he saw few people actually turn from Islam to Christianity, his love and respect for Muslims greatly helped to pave the way for sharing Jesus with Muslims today.

In 1929, at age 62, he became the chairman of history of religion and Christian missions at Princeton University. He continued to write and speak through the rest of his life.

Zwemer's life was filled with difficulties, but he always enjoyed having fun and joking. He was even known to laugh loudly in restaurants!

He later taught at Biblical Seminary in New York and the Missionary Training Institute at Nyack, New York. At age 85, after a full life of service for Christ, this "apostle to Islam" went to be with the Lord.

Zwemer envisioned a day when many in the Islamic world would put their faith in Christ. Faithful Christian workers who had "thrown out the net" with little response would be rewarded with a great ingathering.

"By faith as we obey our Lord's commission," he said, "the time will come when Muslims will be brought to Christ in such numbers that the boats (or churches) will not be able to hold them."[3]

Today, the Samuel Zwemer Institute continues work among Muslims. As one friend observed, Zwemer was "a man of one idea. While his interests and knowledge was wide, I never talked to him ten minutes that the conversation did not veer to Islam."[4]

HOW NOW SHOULD WE LIVE?

What will you do with the treasure-trove of greatness you've discovered?

Warren Wiersbe cautions, "We must never, after reading a biography of a great man, merely imitate him. . . . But each of us can learn from the lives of those whom God has singularly gifted and used. To quote Brooks[1] again, 'The object of reading biography . . . is not imitation but inspiration.' "[2]

While we are inspired by the greatness of these servants of Christ, it's important to remember that, like us, they were imperfect. Even the great prophet Elijah "was just as human as we are" (James 5:17; Contemporary English Version). It should be comforting to realize that this collection includes both extroverts and introverts, Calvinists and Arminians, men and women. Some were notably eccentric. Others were so plain that only their colossal exploits set them apart.

Also, be advised that greatness is a sure magnet for enemies. If you dare defy the status quo you will pay a price. It is probably true that the higher one rises the more polarizing he or she becomes. Great people are ardently loved and vehemently hated.

For those great lives chronicled here, the resistance of detractors was augmented by warfare against the powers of darkness, demonic hordes Paul calls "the spiritual forces of evil in the heavenly realms" (Eph. 6:12; NIV). Satan never concedes one inch to God's kingdom without a fight. Also, several of these great ones struggled with relationships. Some led tornadic lives that left debris of wounded, disappointed workers, friends, and even family members.

Further, we dare not sweep under the rug the fact that often their families paid an enormous price. Regrettably, some of these great ones frequently placed "the ministry" above their families. Yet others had families who fared very well. God is not calling us to win the world and in the process lose our own children. But I have known those who so enshrined family life and were so protective of "quality time" that the children never saw the kind of consuming love that made their parents' faith attractive to them. Some have lost their children, not because they weren't at their soccer games or didn't take family vacations, but because they never transmitted a loyalty to Jesus that went deep enough to interrupt personal preferences.

While the lives of those great for God may sometimes caution us, far more often their lives beckon us to dream greater and reach higher than we may have ever dared. What exactly should you *do* with this new information and inspiration? It is my ardent prayer that you will act. No doubt you have been moved by what you've read. Maybe you've even been shaken. The issue, however, is, *will you change?* Will your heart, your mind — and most importantly — your will so interplay with these stories that you take decisive steps toward your destiny? Will you be great for God?

There are crucial takeaways from these lives that we can grasp. Several vital traits keep cropping up in all these great lives — virtues they shared that, if we would be great for God, must now be ours as well. What lessons do these extraordinary servants of Christ teach us?

Love. Their lives were driven by love for Christ (see 2 Cor. 5:14). This love drove them to their lives' callings and kept them sturdy through storms. As Elisabeth Elliot cogently observed, "The love of Christ constrains us. There is no other motivation for missionary service that is going to survive the blows of even the first year. You do it for *Him*."[3]

For them, love and loyalty were linked. Jesus said, "If you love Me, keep My commandments" (John 14:15). These great ones did not aspire to greatness, they aspired to obedience. Foremost for them, this meant obeying His command to take the gospel to the world and make disciples of all nations.

Yet even in these noble lives, human love had its limits. That is when the love *of* Christ literally took over. They allowed the Holy Spirit to produce His fruit and at the center of that beautiful cluster is love (see Gal. 5:22–23). This isn't just our love; it is His love flowing through us.

Intimacy. Their love for the Lord was nurtured by simply spending time with Him and saying yes to His promptings. Most often, they received these marching orders in a vigilantly kept habit of daily devotions. As I have researched the lives of each person spotlighted in this book, I've concluded that for every one of them daily time in God's presence was a rigorously observed high priority. This practice is the most commonly held trait in this collection of very diverse lives. For almost all of them, this spiritual discipline was their first activity each day. This signaled the value they placed on this "Morning Watch"; they saw it as a kind of "first fruits" offering (see Ps. 5:3, 63:1). This was not some doleful religious exercise. It wasn't legalism, it was loyalty.

John R. Mott contended that this singular discipline was a great key to high impact. "In the proper observance of this watch, more than in any other habit, is to be found the secret of triumphant life and fruitful service," he wrote. "No price is too great for the worker to pay in order to make the Morning Watch a great reality in his life."[4]

Sally Magnusson, Eric Liddell's biographer, notes, "[Eric] seemed to get his strength and self-discipline and air of quiet serenity from his early morning sessions of prayer, meditation, and Bible study. . . . Whatever he received in those morning sessions he spent the rest of the day giving out to others. He measured his standards by it, and if he thought those standards had slipped, he was as stern with himself as he declined to be with others. Somewhere in this daily discipline of faith lay the secret of the man, perhaps the secret of how he ran."[5]

Focus. Though their lives were full of activity, they were not frivolous. Their work was deliberate and purposeful. They didn't "beat the air" (1 Cor. 9:26). Whatever they were doing, it somehow tied to turning Jesus' foes into His friends and His friends into His ardent followers. When they interacted with those who didn't know Christ they were intentionally evangelistic. When they ministered to believers they intentionally moved them toward maturity as His disciples. The sum of their days was all about the glory of God and fulfilling the Great Commission.

Their lives and ministries were so intertwined that often man and message seemed one entity; idea and individual became a single package. All work carried its own dignity and urgency because it was part of a kingdom agenda. As Reggie McNeal observes, those who are great for God "feel personally responsible for partnering with God in his mission. They may work in very obscure places, but changing the world is their aim. This concern is not fitted in around the edges of life; it is the preoccupation of the called."[6] They lived for what matters — the exaltation of God's Son to the ends of the earth.

Calling. These days we hear a lot of talk about destiny. Almost always, this refers to *my* destiny with little or no reference to the larger scheme of things. Such was not the case with these great lives. They saw their calling as part of an unfolding drama — God's determined purpose to bring worldwide worship to His Son. Their lives had intrinsic purpose because they were caught up in God's big plan. Therefore, they had a well-defined sense of destiny and confidence in their calling. This didn't foster pride, however. Rather, it spawned a humble amazement that God would allow them the privilege of partnering with Him. These great ones had a clear understanding of their position and authority in Christ, yet they did not emit a spirit of entitlement.

Vision. In our day we have produced visionary heavyweights and character bantamweights. But for these great ones, their great vision was bolstered by great character. Their great achievements were often simply a Spirit-sensitized conscience replying to a glaring injustice. Vision was born out of burden. Their calling to re-demptively remake some broken situation fueled a clear vision. In the midst of crushing challenges they were upheld by a biblical vi-sion of Christ's triumph.

Because they literally felt called by God, they also felt a keen responsibility to turn their vision into reality. "We have the oppor-tunity to do larger things," wrote John R. Mott, "and we are going to be judged by our talents and the use of them. God forbid that we should lack vision in these days to take advantage of the tide that is rising to sweep multitudes into the all-embracing kingdom of Jesus Christ."[7]

Parallel with the vision of their work was a sanctified imagi-nation. For instance, when William Carey encountered a barren wilderness, he proceeded to plant forests, introduce gardens, teach husbandry, and establish forums such as the Agri-Horticultural So-ciety of India. These great ones were not paralyzed by asking *why?* Rather, they were energized by asking *why not?*

Faith. This leads us to a premier reason for their greatness — they exercised ferocious faith. Theirs was not the docile, generic "faith" that is touted today even by secularists. Their faith had an object. Their faith knew how to fight (see 1 Tim. 6:12). They were convinced of the transforming power of the gospel (see Rom. 1:16). Their confidence in God and His promises forced them to press on. "We have heard of many people who trusted God too little," Hudson Taylor said, "but have you ever heard of anyone who trusted Him too much?"[8]

Biblical faith is separate from (and often juxtaposed against) self-confidence or merely a can-do attitude. These great ones knew their weaknesses, including their deficiencies of faith. Sometimes doubts would lurk on the fringes of faith. At other times, there was all-out conflict as fear and doubt sought to destroy faith. Still, they stood their ground. They would rather have died in faith than lived in unbelief. They echoed Job's confession, "Though He slay me, yet will I trust Him" (Job 13:15).

Their lives were *soli Deo gloria* — only for the glory of God. I've stressed throughout this book that they were great *for God*. In the same way, they had faith first *in God*, not in their own abilities. With

Carey, these great ones expected great things from God. He is, after all, omnipotent.

Work. Faith drove them to act — and act decisively. Since they expected great things from God they attempted great things for Him. There was consistency in their work, for they saw work as a form of worship. There was also urgency in their work, for they legitimately felt that their actions could make the difference in the eternal destiny of multitudes.

These great ones were driven to colossal output because they carried a sense of urgency. They knew they had to seize opportunities "while it is day; the night is coming when no one can work" (John 9:4). The Bible taught them to "make the most of every opportunity" (Eph. 5:16; NIV). A missions anthem expressed their commitment:

> Work for the night is coming,
> > work through the sunny noon;
> Fill brightest hours with labor,
> > rest comes sure and soon.
> Give every flying minute
> > something to keep in store;
> Work for the night is coming,
> > when man works no more.[9]

It is true that no amount of hard work will compensate for lack of anointing. It is equally true that no amount of anointing will compensate for a lack of hard work. Although the great ones we have read about were staunchly Protestant, they would have agreed with the Catholic belief that sloth is a deadly sin. (Today we have softened the bluntness of this destiny destroyer with the term *procrastination.*) When Jesus taught the disciples about the great spiritual harvest, He said to pray for more workers — not observers, not critics — *workers* (see Matt. 9:38).

To cite Carey once again, he saw himself primarily as a worker, a plodder. Carey's biographers noted, "For him, 'work' was not merely a job or a career, but a means of establishing human dominion over the material realm . . . a means of partially realizing God's image in ourselves. The evangelicals of Carey's generation were convinced that we become less of God's image when we choose to be lazy. Many of them wrote daily journals and, if they thought that they had wasted time on a particular day they repented. Wasting time, not being diligent in work, were serious moral issues for them."[10]

Courage. Someone has noted that the pioneers are the guys that have arrows in their backs. They are willing to be maligned in their own generation to build a road for coming generations. The prophets that one generation kills are honored by the statues their children erect.

Think of Mary, the courageous mother of Jesus. She believed God would do something through her that had never happened in all history. Knowing full well the risks to her reputation and future, she said yes to God's high call on her life. She was willing to suffer the sneers of scoffers in her own lifetime because she knew that "henceforth all generations will call me blessed" (Luke 1:48).

Long before they forged remote rivers, walked with children all night through hostile territory, or risked bringing the gospel to unreached tribes, these great ones had already laid down their lives. They had already settled the martyr issue; it was a potential for each of them. Like the heroes of biblical times, "they did not love their lives to the death" (Rev. 12:11). Having laid down their very lives, all other calls to courage were answered swiftly. The default button was already set on *Obey*. Galatians 2:20 was not merely a theological tenet for them, it was daily experience. They didn't just exhibit faith; they displayed *daring, high-risk* faith.

They were convinced that God had given them a pre-set number of days. Because their times were literally in His hands, they could take risks for God (see Ps. 31:15). A hymn most of them would have known summoned them:

> Where duty calls, or danger,
> Be never wanting there.[11]

They were never to be "wanting" in the face of fear because they could draw on supernatural resources for courage. Another missions hymn assured them:

Anywhere, anywhere! Fear I cannot know;
Anywhere with Jesus I can safely go.[12]

Self-denial. Jesus taught that self-denial is Step One in discipleship. "If anyone desires to come after Me," He said, "let him deny himself, take up his cross daily, and follow Me" (Luke 9:23). These days we hear much about self-realization and self-fulfillment. Denying oneself anything (except to enhance beauty or excel in sports) is often viewed negatively in our consumer culture. Yet those who give their lives away in service to God and others end up far more self-fulfilled and self-realized than those who sought these as ends in themselves. For them, self-denial was a potent asset. Since the nexus of their lives was God and others, they indeed "forgot themselves into greatness."[13] With the Apostles, they saw themselves as servants of Christ (Rom 1:1; Phil. 1:1; Titus 1:1; James 1:1; 2 Pet. 1:1). With their Lord, they "did not come to be served, but to serve" (Mark 10:45).

Daily humbling oneself before the Lord is a way of life for those who are great for God. God's enabling grace is dispensed as a result (1 Pet. 5:5). This humble heart-attitude was expressed powerfully in one of Bob Pierce's frequent, dangerous prayers: "Lord, I give you license to interfere in my life and plans at any time, in any way, at any cost to me."[14] With eyes wide open they chose to "fall on the rock" and be broken (Luke 20:18).

These great ones had a healthy view of their humanity, a combination of self-affirmation and self-denial. As theologian John Stott wrote, they lived "affirming everything in us that comes to us from our creation and redemption and denying everything that can be traced to the Fall."[15] They possessed anointing without arrogance, boldness without brashness, power without pride.

Eternity. They lived with an eternal perspective. For them, the supreme payoff was to hear Jesus' affirming *well done* over their lives.

Here lies a great key to their tenacity. If viewed in the light of eternity, even the most painful challenges can be seen as "light afflictions" and the most difficult problems can be viewed as "but for a moment" (2 Cor. 4:17). No matter what the struggle, they knew they were literally being watched and that their response was being recorded. God would not forget their labor of love (Heb. 6:10). Saints of earlier eras were cheering them on (Heb. 12:1–2).

Knowing that they would give an account of their lives and ministries to the Lord helped them tie each day's work to the big picture (Rom. 14:10; 2 Cor. 5:10). They lived each day in light of That Day. They knew that what they were doing that day would matter a thousand years from that day. As 21-year-old Jim Elliot wrote, "There's work to be done, and skilled laborers are needed to complete the building of God. May He grant that I be one of them. What greater privilege than to be able to aid in presenting a glorious Church to such a worthy Redeemer?"[16]

Supernatural. Several of these soft-spoken heroes literally shook and reshaped nations. All of them profoundly influenced the church. How could such incredible spiritual feats be accomplished? "'Not by might nor by power, but by My Spirit,' says the LORD of hosts" (Zech. 4:6). "All God's giants have been weak men," declared Hudson Taylor, "who did great things for God because they reckoned on His being with them."[17] They took Jesus' promise at face value: "He who believes in Me, the works that I do he will do also; and greater works than these he will do, because I go to My Father" (John 14:12).

They expected miracles and divine intervention. It was natural, they believed, for Christians to have God's touch not only on their character but on their careers. Hudson Taylor declared, "We are a supernatural people born again by a supernatural birth, kept by a supernatural power; sustained on supernatural food, taught by a supernatural Teacher from a supernatural Book. We are led by a supernatural Captain in right paths to assured victories."[18]

These were men and women who simply gave a great God opportunity to do great things. Because they walked with God they were strong and carried out great exploits (Dan. 8:32). They lived in what Bob Pierce called "God room": "Nothing is a miracle until it reaches that area where the very utmost that human effort can do is not enough and God moves in to fill that space between what is possible and *what He wants done that is impossible* — that is 'God room.' "[19]

Hope. Faith, hope, and love are abiding core values for believers (1 Cor. 13:13). We hear a good deal of teaching about faith and love, as well we should. But in our day it is equally necessary to have a biblically rooted theology of hope. If hope evaporates, faith and love will not be far behind.

These great ones nurtured their hope in an eschatology that assured them Jesus would write the final chapter of history. This was not flimsy, humanistic optimism; this was biblically grounded hope. It went far deeper than just an upbeat attitude. Great missions hymns like "Jesus Shall Reign" assured them that one day Christ would rule unrivaled over every people and nation. Therefore, they prayed large prayers — and got large answers. Even with their failings and limitations, as Bruce Wilkinson writes, "like those Christians in the Book of Acts — [they] look at who they are and who they'll never be, and what they can do now and what they'll never be able to do . . . and still ask God for the world."[20] Their lives exuded significance because they were Christ's emissaries for shaping history (2 Cor. 5:20). They were world changers.

They refused to be spiritually paralyzed simply because they lacked money, resources, or influence. No matter how dire the situation, they were "prisoners of hope" (Zech. 9:12). Even after years of unrelenting work and little fruit William Carey brimmed with hope. He wrote:

> When I left England, my hope of India's conversion was very strong; but amongst so many obstacles, it would die, unless upheld by God. Well, I have God, and His Word is true. Though the superstitions of the heathen were a thousand times stronger than they are, and the example of the Europeans a thousand times worse; though I were deserted by all and persecuted by all, yet my faith, fixed on the sure Word, would rise above all obstructions and overcome every trial. God's cause will triumph.[21]

What a lesson for our day.

Examining these 12 traits is something of a "de-coding" of their greatness; a separating of strands within their spiritual DNA. There is value in identifying each component but the uniqueness is in the composite. You will find these strands in the spiritual DNA of all who are great for God. And here's the good news — the activity of the same Spirit who transformed them can bring these virtues to the forefront in your life. These lives eloquently teach that a truly successful life is measured not by its duration but by its direction; not by its parties but by its purpose; not by the embracing of things but by embracing the One Thing — to love Jesus supremely and to make Him loved by people everywhere.

As this book ends, your challenge begins. New chapters must be written. New heroes must join the ranks of heaven's Hall of Fame. The King of all nations summons you to greatness — for His glory and the extending of His kingdom. History awaits your response.

Endnotes

INTRODUCTION

1. Sermon by J.F.K. Studd in Keith Hunt and Gladys M. Hunt, *For Christ and the University* (Downers Grove, IL: InterVarsity Press, 1991), p. 40.
2. http://www.wmcarey.edu/carey/expect/expect.htm.
3. Francis Bacon, "Of Studies," *Essays* (1597).
4. James Emery White, *Serious Times: Making Your Life Matter in an Urgent Day* (Downers Grove, IL: InterVarsity Press, 2004), p. 49.
5. Robert Frost, "The Road Not Taken" (1920).
6. From the title of the classic devotional by Oswald Chambers, *My Utmost for His Highest*.
7. See *Living as if Heaven Matters* by David Shibley (Lake Mary, FL: Charisma House, 2007).

CHAPTER 1 — ROWLAND BINGHAM

Opening quote: www.proverbs2525.org/collections/quotes_missions.php
Pull quote: J.H. Hunter, *A Flame of Fire: The Life and Work of R.V. Bingham* (Scarborough, Ontario: Sudan Interior Mission, 1961), p. 111.

1. Ruth A. Tucker, *From Jerusalem to Irian Jaya* (Grand Rapids, MI: Zondervan Publishing House, 1983), p. 296.

CHAPTER 2 — BILL BRIGHT

Opening quote: Randal Roberts, General Editor, *Lessons in Leadership* (Grand Rapids, MI: Kregel Publications, 1999), 54.
Pull quote: Michael Richardson, *Amazing Faith: The Authorized Biography of Bill Bright* (Colorado Springs: WaterBrook Press, 2000), p. 263.

1. Ibid., p. 11.
2. Ibid., p. 15–16.
3. Betty Lee Skinner, *Daws: The Story of Dawson Trotman* (Grand Rapids, MI: Zondervan Books, 1974), p. 190, 350.
4. Wendy Murray Zoba, "Bill Bright's Wonderful Plan for the World, Part 2," *Christianity Today,* posted July 17, 1997, accessed December 28, 2011.
5. Statistics are from http://billbrightccci.org/public, accessed December 23, 2011.
6. Richardson, *Amazing Faith: The Authorized Biography of Bill Bright*, p. xii.
7. Zoba, "Bill Bright's Wonderful Plan for the World, Part 2," accessed December 28, 2011.
8. Statistics from www.jesusfilm.org, accessed December 28, 2011.
9. www.ccci.org, accessed December 28, 2011.
10. David Shibley, *A Force in the Earth* (Lake Mary, FL: Creation House, 1997), p. 98.

11. Ron Luce interview with Bill Bright, July 2003.
12. Bill Bright, *The Journey Home* (Nashville, TN: Thomas Nelson Publishers, 2003), p. 3.
13. Ibid., p. 22.
14. www.sermonscentral.com, accessed December 22, 2011.

CHAPTER 3 — WILLIAM CAREY
Opening/Pull quote: Sermon to Baptist Ministers, Nottingham, England, 1792.
1. Leon McBeth, *Men Who Made Missions* (Nashville, TN: Broadman Press, 1968), p. 79.
2. Ibid.
3. Robert Hall tribute to William Carey, June 9, 1834.

CHAPTER 4 — AMY CARMICHAEL
Opening quote: Quoted from *The Journals of Jim Elliot* in Elisabeth Elliot, *Shadow of the Almighty: The Life and Testament of Jim Elliot* (New York: Harper & Brothers, 1958), 15.
Pull quote: Elisabeth Elliot, *A Chance to Die* (Grand Rapids, MI: Fleming H. Revell, 1987), p. 264.
1. Sherwood Eddy, *Pathfinders of the World Missionary Crusade* (Nashville, TN: Abingdon-Cokesbury, 1945), p. 263.
2. Elliot, *A Chance to Die: The Life and Legacy of Amy Carmichael*, p. 25–26.
3. V. Raymond Edman, *They Found the Secret* (Grand Rapids, MI: Zondervan Publishing House, 1960), p. 38.
4. Elliot, *A Chance to Die*, p. 264.

CHAPTER 5 — JIM ELLIOT
Opening/Pull quote: Elisabeth Elliot, *Shadow of the Almighty: The Life & Testament of Jim Elliot* (New York: Harper & Brothers, 1958), p. 15.
1. Ibid., p. 247.
2. Ibid., p. 39.
3. *The Journals of Jim Elliot*, edited by Elizabeth Elliot (Ada, MI: Revell, 2002).
4. Quoted in Elliot, *Shadow of the Almighty*, p. 248.
5. Ibid., p. 121.
6. Ibid., p. 132.
7. Ibid., p. 236.
8. *Auca* is the Quichua word for savage. Today this indigenous people group are known as the Huaorani or Waodoni.
9. Elliot, *Shadow of the Almighty*, p. 232.
10. Cited in Daniel P. Fuller, *Give the Winds a Mighty Voice: The Story of Charles E. Fuller* (Waco, TX: Word Books, 1972), p. 188.

CHAPTER 6 — CHARLES E. FULLER
Opening/Pull quote: Daniel P. Fuller, *Give the Winds a Mighty Voice: The Story of Charles E. Fuller* (Waco, TX: Word Books, 1972), p. 188.
1. Fuller, *Give the Winds a Mighty Voice*, p. 34.
2. Ibid., p. 238.
3. Ibid., p. 88.

CHAPTER 7 — H.B. GARLOCK
Opening/Pull quote: H.B. Garlock and Ruthanne Garlock, *Before We Kill and Eat You* (Dallas, TX: Christ for the Nations Publishing, 1974).
1. Ibid., p. 44–45.
2. Ibid., p. 89–90.
3. www.church313.com, accessed December 11, 2011.

CHAPTER 8 — ADONIRAM JUDSON
Opening/Pull quote: Arthur Judson Brown, *The Foreign Missionary: An Incarnation of a World Movement* (New York: Fleming H. Revell Publishers, 1932), p. 374.
1. Ibid., p. 374.

CHAPTER 9 — ERIC LIDDELL
Opening/Pull quote: Mark Harris, "The Flying Man," *Mission Frontiers* (November–December 2008): p. 6.
1. Eric Liddell, *The Disciplines of the Christian Life* (Nashville, TN: Abingdon Press, 1985), p. 21.
2. Katrina von Schlegel (b. 1697), "Be Still My Soul," translated by Jane L. Borthwick (1813–1897).
3. Dr. David J. Mitchell, "Recollections of Eric Liddell," http://www.ericliddell.org/eric-liddell/recollections/davidmitchell.html.
4. Sally Magnusson, *The Flying Scotsman* (New York: Quartet Books, 1981), p. 165.

CHAPTER 10 — PAUL LITTLE
Opening/Pull quote: Rick Richardson, "Evangelism in InterVarsity," www.intervasity.org/evangelism/article_item.php7article_id=1599, accessed December 11, 2011.
1. Paul E. Little, "The God Who Never Lets Things Just Happen," *Moody Monthly* (June 1975): p. 42–44.

CHAPTER 11 — DAVID LIVINGSTONE
Opening/Pull quote: www.urbana.org/cloud-of-witnesses/explorer-missionary, accessed December 11, 2011.
1. Oliver Bansford, *David Livingstone: The Dark Interior* (New York: St. Martin's Press, 198), p. 14.
2. W. Garden Blaikie, *The Personal Life of David Livingstone* (New York, NY: Fleming H. Revell Publishers, 1880), p. 29.

CHAPTER 12 — LOTTIE MOON

Opening/Pull quote: Tungchow, China, September 15, 1887, www.pbcmar-seilles.com/message.php7messageID=10748&, accessed December 11, 2011.

1. Tucker, *From Jerusalem to Irian Jaya*, p. 234.
2. Ibid., p. 235–236.
3. Ibid., p. 237.
4. Ibid.

CHAPTER 13 — JOHN R. MOTT

Opening/Pull quote: "The Responsibility of the Young People for the Evangelization of the World," *Missionary Issues of the Twentieth Century* (1901), *Perspectives on the World Christian Movement*, third edition (Pasadena, CA: William Carey Library, 1999), p. 322.

1. John R. Mott, *The Evangelization of the World in This Generation* (New York, NY: Student Volunteer Movement for Foreign Missions, 1900), p. 19.
2. Basil Matthews, *John R. Mott: World Citizen* (New York: Harper & Brothers Publishers, 1934), p. 168.
3. John R. Mott, *The Present World Situation* (New York: Student Volunteer Movement for Foreign Missions, 1914), p. 208–209, cited in Martha Smalley, *The Legacy of John R. Mott*, Occasional Publication, No. 3 (New Haven, CT: Yale Divinity School Library, 1993), p. 16.
4. Cited by Lon Allison, *That the World May Believe* (Wheaton, IL: EMIS, 2002), p. 23.
5. Ibid., p. 25.
6. Matthews, *John R. Mott: World Citizen*, p. x.
7. Mott, *The Evangelization of the World in This Generation*, p. 19.
8. C. Howard Hopkins, *John R. Mott: A Biography* (Grand Rapids, MI: William B. Eerdmans Publishing Company, 1979), p. 703.
9. Ibid., p. 684.

CHAPTER 14 — BOB PIERCE

Opening/Pull quote: Tucker, *From Jerusalem to Irian Jaya*, p. 468.

1. Franklin Graham with Jeanette Lockerbie, *Bob Pierce: This One Thing I Do* (Waco, TX: Word Books Publ., 1983), p. 40.
2. Ibid., p. 41–42.
3. Ibid., p. 77.
4. Ibid., p. 56
5. Ibid., p. 149.
6. Marilee Pierce Dunker, *Man of Vision, Woman of Prayer* (Nashville, TN: Thomas Nelson Publishers, 1980), p. 252.
7. Graham with Lockerbie, *Bob Pierce*, p. 217.

CHAPTER 15 — WARREN SHIBLEY
Opening/Pull quote: David Shibley, editor, *Challenging Quotes for World Changers* (Green Forest, AR: New Leaf Press, 1995), p. 108.
1. www.osborn.org.

CHAPTER 16 — MARY SLESSOR
Opening/Pull quote: www.wholesomewords.org/missions/msquotes.html, accessed December 11, 2011.
1. W.P. Livingstone, *Mary Slessor: The White Queen* (London: Hodder & Stoughton, Ltd., 1931), p. 21–22.
2. Ibid., p. 29.

CHAPTER 17 — OSWALD J. SMITH
Opening/Pull quote: Oswald J. Smith, *The Passion for Souls* (London: Marshall, Morgan & Scott, 1964), p. 45.
1. Lois Neely, *Fire in His Bones: The Official Biography of Oswald J. Smith* (Wheaton, IL: Tyndale House Publishers, 1982), p. 63.
2. Ibid., p. 231–232.
3. Ibid., p. 171.
4. Ibid., p. 219.
5. Ibid., p. 278.
6. Ibid., p. 296.
7. Ibid.

CHAPTER 18 — C. T. STUDD
Opening/Pull quote: www.wholesomewords.org/missions/msquotes.html, accessed December 11, 2011.
1. Tucker, *From Jerusalem to Irian Jaya*, p. 315.
2. http://quotationsbook.com/quote/6637.

CHAPTER 19 — HUDSON TAYLOR
Opening/Pull quote: Andrew Murray, *Key to the Missionary Problem,* contemporized by Leona Choy (Fort Washington, PA: Christian Literature Crusade, 1979), p. 88.
1. Tucker, *From Jerusalem to Irian Jaya*, p. 173.
2. Hudson Taylor, *Hudson Taylor, The Autobiography* (Minneapolis, MN: Bethany House Publishers), p. 12.
3. Ibid., p. 21.
4. Edman, *They Found the Secret*, p. 18.
5. http://www.goodreads.com/author/quotes/594568.J_Hudson_Taylor, accessed January 4, 2012.
6. Henry W. Frost, "Characteristics of Hudson Taylor," *China's Millions* (May 1932): p. 68–70.
7. Ibid., p, 70.

CHAPTER 20 — WILLIAM CAMERON TOWNSEND

Opening/Pull quote: James Hefley and Marti Hefley, *Uncle Cam* (Milford, MI: Mott Media, 1981), p. 182.

1. Ibid., p. 67.
2. Clarence W. Hall, *Adventurers for God*, "Two Thousand Tongues" (New York, NY: Harper and Brothers, 1959), p. 119.
3. Hefley and Hefley, *Uncle Cam*, p. 251.
4. Ibid., p. 182.

CHAPTER 21 — DAWSON TROTMAN

Opening/Pull quote:. Betty Lee Skinner, *Daws: The Story of Dawson Trotman* (Grand Rapids, MI: Zondervan Publishing House, 1974), 35

1. Ibid., p. 29.
2. Ibid., p. 30.
3. Ibid., p. 35.
4. Dawson Trotman, *The Need of the Hour* (Colorado Springs, CO: NavPress), booklet.
5. "Religion: The Navigator," *Time* magazine, July 2, 1956.

CHAPTER 22 — NIKOLAUS LUDWIG VON ZINZENDORG

Opening/Pull quote: Quoted by John Piper, "At the Price of God's Own Blood," May 7, 1989, www.blubrry.com/.../at-the-price-of-gods-own-blood-by-john-piper.

1. www.bswe.org/resources/missions-quotes.

CHAPTER 23 — SAMUEL ZWEMER

Opening/Pull quote: Samuel Zwemer, *The Unoccupied Mission Fields of Africa and Asia* (Student Volunteer Movement for Foreign Missions, 1911), *Perspectives on the World Christian Movement,* fourth edition (Pasadena, CA: William Carey Library, 2009), p. 322.

1. http://www.quotationspage.com/quote/2815.html.
2. Ralph D. Winter and Steven C. Hawthorne, editors, *Perspectives on the World Christian Movement,* "The Glory of the Impossible," Samuel Zwemer (Pasadena, CA: William Carey Library, 1981), p. 254.
3. J. Christy Wilson Jr., "The Apostle to Islam: The Legacy of Samuel Zwemer," *International Journal of Frontier Missions*, vol. 13:4 (Oct.–Dec. 1996), p. 166.
4. Winter and Hawthorne, *Perspectives on the World Christian Movement*, p. 253.

AFTERWORD

1. Phillips Brooks, renowned Boston pastor who wrote the lyrics to the Christmas carol, "O Little Town of Bethlehem."
2. Warren Wiersbe, *Walking With the Giants* (Grand Rapids, MI: Baker Book House, 1976), p. 15–16.

3. David Shibley, editor, *Challenging Quotes for World Changers* (Green Forest, AR: New Leaf Press, 1995), p. 86.

4. Basil Matthews, *John R. Mott: World Citizen* (New York: Harper & Brothers Publishers, 1934), p. 378.

5. Sally Magnusson, *The Flying Scotsman: A Biography* (New York: Quartet Books, 1981), p. 104.

6. Reggie McNeal, *A Work of Heart* (San Francisco, CA: Jossey-Bass Publishers, 2000), p. 98.

7. Winter and Hawthorne, *Perspectives on the World Christian Movement,* p. 320.

8. Helen Hossier, editor, *The Quotable Christian* (Uhrichsville, OH: Barbour Publishing, 1998), p. 206.

9. Anna Coghill, "Work for the Night Is Coming" (1854).

10. Vishal & Ruth Mangalwadi, *The Legacy of William Carey: A Model for the Transformation of a Culture* (Wheaton, IL: Crossway Books, 1999), p. 116.

11. George Duffield Jr., "Stand Up, Stand Up for Jesus" (1858).

12. Jessie Pounds, "Anywhere with Jesus" (1887).

13. See E. Stanley Jones, *Abundant Living* (Nashville, TN: Abingdon Press, 1942), p. 11–12.

14. Graham with Lockerbie, *Bob Pierce: This One Thing I Do*, p. 11–12.

15. John Stott, *The Radical Disciple* (Downers Grove, IL: InterVarsity Press, 2010), p. 26.

16. *The Journals of Jim Elliot*, November 16, 1948.

17. *Hudson Taylor's Choice Sayings: A Compilation from His Writings and Addresses* (London: China Inland Mission, n.d.), p. 29.

18. Hudson Taylor, cited in Andrew Murray, *Key to the Missionary Problem* contemporized by Leona Choy (Fort Washington, PA: Christian Literature Crusade, 1979), p. 88.

19. Graham with Lockerbie, *Bob Pierce: This One Thing I Do*, p. 52–53.

20. Bruce Wilkinson, *The Prayer of Jabez* (Sisters, OR: Multnomah Publishers, 2000), p. 6.

21. http://www.goodreads.com/quotes/show/384040.

MORE FROM DAVID SHIBLEY

David Shibley is founder and international representative of *Global Advance*, a ministry providing training, resources, and encouragement to church and marketplace leaders worldwide. Founded in 1990, Global Advance provides on-site training to tens of thousands of leaders each year throughout the Majority World (developing countries around the globe). Since its founding Global Advance has brought face-to-face training to some 600,000 Christian leaders in 81 nations. David has ministered in 52 nations in conferences, churches, and evangelistic outreaches. Also, he ministers extensively throughout the United States, challenging the American church to reach its full mission potential.

Raised in a pastor's home, world missions has been a central theme of David's life and ministry. The vision of Global Advance is to equip one million pastoral leaders and one million business leaders *("the Marketplace Million")* in the Majority World to impact their nations for Christ. A major emphasis for David is mentoring young men in ministry. He has been interviewed on several Christian television network programs including *The 700 Club, TBN* and *Daystar*. He has served on the boards of eight ministries and currently serves with the Strategy Working Group for the Lausanne Movement.

David is the author of numerous articles and 21 books including the acclaimed mission classics, *A Force in the Earth* and *The Missions Addiction*. He honors the work of some of history's most influential and unforgettable missionaries and mission leaders in *Great for God*. He is a graduate of John Brown University in Arkansas *(where he was named the Outstanding Alumnus of the Year in 1995)* and Southwestern Baptist Theological Seminary. He also received an honorary doctorate from Oral Roberts University. He and his wife, Naomi, have been married since 1972 and have two married sons and five grandchildren.

For more information regarding Global Advance and David Shibley, contact:

GLOBAL ADVANCE
P.O. Box 742077
Dallas, TX 75374-2077
972.771.9042

www.globaladvance.org
www.davidshibley.com
facebook.com/**Davidshibley**
facebook.com/**GreatforGod**

Other books by David Shibley from New Leaf Press

Now That You Are His

Marketplace Memos
(with Jonathan Shibley)